ENDORSEMENTS

The trauma many women have from abortion has permanently scarred them for life, but this book proves it can be healed! A MUST READ!

SID ROTH
Host of *It's Supernatural!*

I am extremely excited to recommend my dear friend Donna Grisham and her life-changing book *Journeys of Choice*. Donna, like few others I know, embodies the cry of Rachel for this generation. She is a voice for the voiceless and one who weeps for a generation that is being led to the slaughter, crying "Choose LIFE!" She possesses a passion for life that is unmatched. Through her story of great loss and despair, you will see how God supernaturally brought new life out of death and has raised her up for such a time as this to be a midwife to an entire generation. She has supernaturally birthed a book that is going to birth many precious babies!

MYLES KILBY
Pastor of The River Church Savannah
Savannah, Georgia

At a recent pro-life rally in North Carolina, protesters shouted, "We will fight. We will win. Throw the fetus in a bin." In this book, you will hear other voices—beautiful voices, restored voices, healed voices—voices of women who chose life, bringing their babies into the world instead of throwing them away. In this day, when death and destruction dominate the news, here is a book filled with life and healing and hope. I pray that, by God's grace, many children's lives will be saved through the testimonies in this book.

DR. MICHAEL L. BROWN
Host of the *Line of Fire* radio program
Author of *Jezebel's War with America*

Journeys of Choice is a must read for everyone! It will change your heart on the issue of abortion as well as your mind. Donna's personal story of the trauma of rape, abortion, and many suicidal attempts until God intervened, as He too will do for you, will change the course of your life. Today, she continues to be a voice for the voiceless and expose the inexcusable lies of the abortion industry. This book not only speaks to the trauma of abortion on the unborn, but also to the devastating impact it has on women and men too. We are so thankful for a book like this, in a time like this!

DAVID & JASON BENHAM
The Benham Brothers

In this powerful book, *Journeys of Choice,* Donna Grisham exposes one of the most diabolical plots in the history of the human race to destroy destiny and steal purpose: abortion. This book is a prophetic clarion call to God's people to loose the shackles of the shame of the past and embrace a bright future...a future filled with hope. This is not a condemnation to those who have committed the sin of abortion, but an eye-opening conversation filled with personal testimonies and personal victories. Anyone who has had an abortion or is considering an abortion or who knows someone who has had an abortion must read this book.

DR. KYNAN BRIDGES
Senior pastor, Grace & Peace Global Fellowship, Inc

Donna Grisham is a voice in this generation who has been tested in the wilderness and carries a fresh anointing from the Holy Spirit. In this incredible book, she details her story of deep brokenness and how out of the ashes comes a beautiful testimony of hope and glory, as well as many other stories. I've had the privilege of being a friend to Donna and can testify that she practices what she has written. Get ready to be blessed; I know I was!

JEREMIAH JOHNSON
Founder of Heart of the Father Ministry
Best-selling author
www.jeremiahjohnson.tv

Many have been deceived and believed lies regarding abortion. In *Journeys of Choice* Donna gives us insights into the truth about abortion and the torments that entrap those involved. We each have a choice to hold onto, cover up, and bury heartbreak and trauma or to allow the Lord to reach into our lives to heal, restore and bring about His purposes. Tragedy and trauma can be a stepping-stone to get us to the next place of our life's journey or it can be a wall that holds us back from God's very best—His destiny for us. Through Donna's openness and the life stories of the others, you will see God's love for you and that He has always had a plan of redemption and restoration for each of us. I encourage you to read *Journeys of Choice* and share it with others. Each life story will bring healing and hope to the brokenhearted. What was meant for evil and harm, God will turn for good and blessings... allow Him to do that for you!

DR. JOHN BENEFIEL
Senior pastor, Church on the Rock
Oklahoma City

One of the greatest privileges one can receive is to endorse the work, word, and character of another. It is in this light that I can personally attest to the work of Donna Grisham, which is superb; her word, which is without fault; and Donna's character, which is without reproach. You will find embedded within her character one who is kind, loving, and compassionate. You will find in her work ethic, the conduct of a superhero. You will find in her word a promise keeper. As you read Donna's book knowing the attributes that it contains within its author, you will, without question, come away knowing truth has been spoken, empathy has been realized, and excellence has been presented.

Donna bares her soul in a unique and transparent way that does not leave any room for the reader to doubt the victory over a very heart-wrenching situation. In sharing intimate details, we find not only the tragedies attached to wrong decisions, but the incredible victory that can only be realized from the heart of a champion who overcame incredible obstacles.

This is a story worth reading, from a life worth living, with a purpose worth sharing with the world.

DR. CLARICE FLUITT
Personal advisor, motivational speaker, author,
and television personality
Founder of Clarice Fluitt Ministries

Throughout *Journeys of Choice*, Donna Grisham inspires while instilling a heavy sense of reality, not just with her own story, but every other story included in this book. These testimonies accurately captivate a deep perspective of very real topics such as abortion and rape that the world wants to normalize. And while the reality of these stories confirm that these things do indeed occur, they also affirm that God is far bigger and stronger than any shame or pain we carry. It is clear that each of these survivors want to help other men and women going through similar shadows. Therefore, I encourage you to read this book and expect to be inspired to conquer any circumstance alongside the living hope that is Jesus.

APOSTLE GUILLERMO MALDONADO
King Jesus International Ministry
Miami, Florida

This book contains the most real, raw, truthful, and transparent testimonies I believe I have ever seen concerning women's as well as men's journey through the heartache of abortion. If you are one of those men or women — or if you know someone — stop the torment and allow God's mercy and grace to penetrate the nightmare and provide a new and beautiful waking dream: a peaceful life full of joy and healing.

PASTOR LAURA HARRIS SMITH, C.N.C.
Nutritionist and author of *Get Well Soon, The Healthy Living Handbook, The 30-Day Faith Detox, Seeing the Voice of God* and more

I know of no one who has been more successful in embracing the teachings of Jesus and encouraging others to do the same. Donna Grisham gives the reader excellent guidelines to make wise choices in their lives. It will bring hope to the hopeless and freedom to the captives. I highly recommend this book to anyone.

PASTOR WILLIAM T LIGON
Brunswick, Georgia

Journeys of Choice is one of the most powerfully inspired books that I have read in a long time. Donna Grisham with each chapter unpacks life-changing stories and testimonies that will literally impart faith into the reader to overcome. This book has interwoven a collection of journeys that is uniquely written to reveal the extraordinary power of choice aligning with God's destiny. Proverbs 19:21 speaks volumes as you read each journey in this book: *"Many are the plans in the mind of a man, but it is the purpose of the Lord that will stand."* Donna epitomizes a true overcomer and survivor who has defied the odds from birth to almost every stage of her life.

As you read the miraculous testimonies in this book there is an anointing of the overcomer released upon the reader. Everyone's journey is different and their choices with God will become their prophetic road map to discover what the prophet Jeremiah has spoken: *"For I know the plans I have for you, declares the Lord. Plans to prosper you and not to harm you, plans to give you a hope and a future"* (Jeremiah 29:11). I highly recommend and endorse this phenomenal book by Donna Grisham for any believer who is ready to decide to go on an extraordinary journey with God.

Dr. Naim Collins
Prophetic Voice
Author of *Realms of the Prophetic*

Journeys of Choice is a book I did not want to put down. I was captivated by the stories in this book; Donna defies the odds stacked up against her and she became an over-comer! *Journeys of Choice* will align your life decisions to the will of God that ultimately will bring you to your purposed destination. Anyone can relate to the content contained in this book in one way or another. We overcome by the word of our testimony and this powerful, life-changing book carries a right now word for healing, restoration, breakthrough. This heartfelt book will inspire, motivate, encourage, and assist you on the road of recovery that will break hope deferred which makes the heart sick, but a dream fulfilled is a tree of life (Prov. 13:12). I recommend this book for anyone ready to DREAM BIG, live again, and encounter the hope of glory found in your daily decisions in God's presence as you journey with Him.

DR. HAKEEM COLLINS
Prophetic voice and international speaker
Author of *Heaven Declares, Prophetic Breakthrough,*
Command Your Healing, and
101 Prophetic Ways God Speaks

In this remarkable work Donna has captured the beautiful and ever gracious heart of God concerning the very sensitive subject of abortion. This book will encourage, inspire, motivate, and most importantly shake the kingdom of darkness. Believers all over the world need to get a copy for themselves and a friend.

TODD SMITH,
Lead Pastor Christ Fellowship Church
Dawsonville, Georgia
Host pastor of the North Georgia Revival

When I was in Heaven, I saw God had books written about us before we were even placed in our mother's womb. We were in God's plan. In this book, I know Donna Grisham shares with you exactly the struggles women go through as well as relatives when it comes to an unplanned pregnancy. This book will show you how important everyone is in God's plan. No matter what decisions you made in your life, whether good or bad, they affect everybody. In *Journeys of Choice*, Donna shows you that no matter how negatively your decisions may have affected people, including your own life, those decisions can be turned around in your life. And you can have a wonderful, fantastic, glorious ending, affecting the lives of many for eternity.

KEVIN and KATHI ZADAI
Warrior Notes Ministries

Journeys
OF
CHOICE

Journeys
OF
CHOICE

THERE IS HOPE IN THE MIDST OF
AN UNPLANNED PREGNANCY

DONNA GRISHAM

DESTINY IMAGE® PUBLISHERS, INC.
P.O. Box 310, Shippensburg, PA 17257-0310
"Promoting Inspired Lives."

This book and all other Destiny Image and Destiny Image Fiction books are available at Christian bookstores and distributors worldwide.

For more information on foreign distributors, call 717-532-3040.
Reach us on the Internet: www.destinyimage.com.

ISBN 13 TP: 978-0-7684-5864-0
ISBN 13 eBook: 978-0-7684-5865-7
ISBN 13 HC: 978-0-7684-5867-1
ISBN 13 LP: 978-0-7684-5866-4

For Worldwide Distribution, Printed in the U.S.A.
3 4 5 6 7 8 / 25 24 23 22 21

DEDICATION

First, I would like to thank God the Father, for without His intervention in my life, I would not be here to see the fruition of this come to pass. You have been my Rock through it all. May Your name be glorified and lives changed because of Your faithfulness in my life.

To my two babies in heaven, daughter Christian Nicole and son Richard David, who were never given the opportunity to live, because of a choice that was made and a fight that was never fought. Your cries of justice will always be heard through my voice and I will never be silent ever again.

My son, Matthew Grisham, a gift given to me that I never deserved. After all I had done, God in His limitless love and compassion trusted you into my care. You, Jackie, and Aaron, my beloved grandson, mean the world to me and I am so thankful for all three of you supporting me during the birthing of this book.

My mother, Ruby Annette Grisham. Forgiveness is beautiful in that no matter what a person has done, when we are open to forgive, God heals the relationship as if the wrong never happened. You became my loudest supporter of doing this book. Your constant encouragement was so refreshing. You may not be on this earth to physically see the fulfilment of this dream, but I know you are with the great cloud of witnesses cheering me onto the finished line. You will forever be in my heart. I love you, Mom.

Ken Brady, my very best friend in the world, who is in heaven watching this all unfold. The many nights we prayed on the phone about this. More than ever you believed in me and you believed in the cause.

Tina Pugh, for believing in me from the beginning when God gave me the vision to write this book. Your constant motivation and inspiration kept me pressing forward. I couldn't have done it without you. Thank you from the bottom of my heart.

Tonya Hildalgo and Connie Janzen, both of you, for helping to keep me in line and for all your help with editing each of the stories. Your willingness to go the extra mile and not give up on me motivated me to not stop until it was done.

To all my friends and family members who prayed for me during this journey. Thank you. Praise God, it's finally finished.

CONTENTS

FOREWORD

MOST FOREWORDS ARE EASY TO WRITE. Although this one was an honor to scribe for my friend Donna Grisham, whom I love and respect, I must admit that every time I sat to type and read through the testimonies within this manuscript, I wept. I wept tears driven by the overwhelming feelings as I am drawn into the realization of the tremendous obstacles and heartbreak each mother faced and walked through. Tears flowed for each one who experienced such trauma. Tears

1

for the precious babies and all lives tragically affected by abortion.

As I read the powerful testimonies of Jeri Hill and Sol Pitchon, my heart rejoiced at the amazing goodness of God. As these lives were spared from abortion, they in turn have been used powerfully to impact so many lives and the world. And praise God that Abby saw the true reality of abortion and quit her job at Planned Parenthood. It is my prayer that the laws of this nation will be changed so that abortion will no longer be legal and Planned Parenthood will be shut down.

Life is a beautiful gift the Lord has freely given to all mankind. All life is precious and beautiful in His sight. He has bestowed to each of us the right, power, and opportunity to choose. Choice is a privilege given to us by God. Therefore, we all face many decisions when we must choose a course of action. Some decisions and choices come easy while others are more difficult. The truth is all our choices affect not only us as individuals but also all of those around us and close to us. So when making a choice, we must think of the long-term ramifications. The following are questions to ask ourselves to provide guidance when decisions are being made: How will the choice I am facing now affect my life? How will it affect those in my life and close to this situation? Is it life giving? Is it righteous or unrighteous? Friends, when it comes to the choice of an unborn life, abortion is not the solution. Why? Because what you see as a problem is a precious treasure and gift in the eyes of the Lord. Even the most unwanted pregnancy can turn into a blessing.

If you are one who has experienced trauma, abuse, or abortion in your past and you are still scarred and hurting, from one woman to another, I encourage you to find a safe haven to receive the ministry of freedom and deliverance to move beyond the pain. The love of our heavenly Father is unending. He is awesome, merciful, forgiving, and beautiful. No matter what trauma and abuse you have experienced, He is always ready to forgive and heal the pain with His magnificent love.

But most importantly, I am honored to be able to step in as a mother and as a Christian to speak to those who are reading this book and who are considering abortion. It is my prayer that you can hear the heart and the voice of the Lord in my words and the power of all the shared testimonies. My plea to you now is the same, "Don't do it!" That precious baby inside of you is a beautifully formed and divinely created life. Our heavenly Father creates no mistakes. Hear me, you are beautiful and are not a mistake. Even if you feel the situation you are in is unplanned, a mistake, or traumatic, that beautiful one nestled inside your womb of safety is not a mistake. Reach out to those safe ones such as Donna, a church, a counselor, a ministry who can help you through this process. Our heavenly Father loves you and that precious one. Jesus loves you. John 10:10 says, *"The thief comes only to steal and kill and destroy; I [Jesus] have come that they may have life, and have it to the full"* (NIV). It is my prayer that you will feel His love in the challenging season and situation you find yourself in. Reach out to Him. Reach out to others who can help. He is so faithful, and He will meet you and walk with you to security and peace.

Donna, thank you for this now word. I am greatly inspired by you and these women and men and the incredible boldness and transparency to share real-life stories about the choices surrounding abortion. Thank you for writing and sharing your story in order to help others. There are so many hurting women, children, and families who have journeyed this path. What is transcribed in this book is a now message. You are a beautiful and bold woman of God. I appreciate and greatly value the ministry the Lord has given you—a voice to the church and the world and most importantly those who are in such desperate need for this word in the moment of decision for life or death. It is my prayer that the message written on the hearts of these women and men highlighted on the pages of *Journeys of Choice* will be highly favored, and those who need it as a now word will find it. I pray that it gets into the hands of government leaders and legislators, and that they will hear the truth of the words and testimonies and resolve to stand for righteousness and justice for the unborn. Now is the time to stand for life.

REBECCA GREENWOOD
Author
Cofounder, Christian Harvest International and
Strategic Prayer Action Network

INTRODUCTION

IN 2015, DURING A RECORDING OF ONE OF THE
It's Supernatural! shows, I was standing next to Sid Roth, the host, as he
waited to greet the audience. The Lord
spoke to me and asked me to write a
book of stories just as Sid had.

Sid Roth wrote a book many
years ago called, *They Thought for
Themselves,* which showcased stories
of different Jewish people who had
received Jesus as their Messiah. My
first thought was, "Well, that's nice,
Lord, but I don't have any stories."

Oh, I had *my* story but no one else's. I had no idea what the title of the book would be or how it was ever going to come together, BUT GOD did! He was at work behind the scenes preparing everything. All He wanted me to do was say yes. After the show, I spoke to Tina Pugh, our Floor Director, and told her what the Lord had said to me. She instantly said that I should contact Jeri Hill and ask her if I could share her story in my book. That night I contacted Jeri to ask her permission to share her story and she said yes. Get ready to be glued to the pages of this book and find out how God took Jeri, a child born out of rape, and now uses her as a life changer for the Kingdom of God.

Soon God started bringing men and women to me with their stories. Each one sharing their experience of coming to a crossroads—making the choice between life and death.

Some asked me, "Donna, what inspired you write a book like this?" Besides just knowing God asked me to write it, and Him wanting me to share my testimony of healing and restoration, deep down I knew there was much more to it. I believe this book is the voice of every baby's cry from inside the womb, and every survivor's voice that was left to die alone yet survived to embrace life at its fullness.

What I've come to realize is that behind the word "choice" is a person.

A real human being that deserves to live—someone's son, daughter, grandchild, brother, sister, niece, nephew, or even someone's spouse.

MELISSA OHDEN
Founder, Abortion Survivors Network

Are you in a situation where you are at the crossroads between the choice of life and the choice of death? What's in your backpack that is weighing you down? Are you fearful of what your future holds? Do you feel as though your life has just stopped or is on hold? I believe this is your moment, it is NOT an accident that you picked up this book. God wants to intervene in your situation and change the course of your life forever if you choose to let Him.

DON'T STOP! KEEP READING! If you are in a situation where you are at the crossroads between the choice of life and the choice of death, you will know that as you choose life God will make a way for you and your baby. If you pray to Him, He will help you make a choice you will never regret. If you have already made that choice, God has His heart open to you and is waiting for you to come to Him. He wants to heal you and set your feet on the path that will lead to an abundant life. After you finish this book it is my prayer that life itself will become more valuable to you on your own journey.

Chapter 1

MY STORY

EVEN IN BIRTH, THE ENEMY WANTED TO SUCK the breath out of a little baby girl, but she would fight to live.

My mom wasn't due to give birth to me for a couple more months. In fact, she wasn't due until Valentine's Day 1960. However, she and dad got into a heated argument, and my mom fell down some stairs, which sent her into premature labor on Sunday, December 13, 1959. She was taken to the Charleston Naval Hospital in South Carolina, and I was born, weighing only two pounds and had little hope of surviving.

I was told that even the doctors were making bets on how much I weighed and whether I would survive. Being born prematurely, especially ten weeks early in 1959, didn't give a baby much of a chance for survival. The neonatal units were not as well equipped as they are today. My mom remembers that things got worse as I began to lose weight and got down to one pound thirteen ounces. She struggled to see how her tiny baby could survive. I was kept in an incubator at the hospital for at least two months, and as the weeks went by, I grew stronger and stronger. I began to fight. The will to live, along with the hand of God on my life, caused this premature little baby girl to defy all the odds. There is no doubt that I was born for such a time as this. To share my story so that others can know that if a one-pound, thirteen-ounce baby can make it against all hope, then every baby should be given the right to live.

The Nightmare Begins

My home life wasn't very pleasant. My dad was in the Navy and was gone most of the time. When he was home, he and my mom fought constantly. My dad was deployed to Vietnam; when he returned, he was not the same man. It became apparent that my mom and dad couldn't live together or be civil to each other, so when I was in the first grade, my dad decided to take me, my older sister, and my brother away from my mother, leaving her on the side of the road with nothing but a suitcase. That picture will be etched in my mind for the rest of my life.

I remember being in the back seat screaming, "I want my mommy," at the top of my lungs. And my dad yelling, "Shut up! Shut up! Stop that crying or I'm going to give you something to cry about!" At that moment, fear gripped me, and I began to live in fear, afraid to do or say anything. Even to this day when going over the bridge in Charleston, I think about it. However, I am thankful that now it is not with the old fear, hurt, and anger I once had. Jesus has healed me from this trauma, and I've been able to forgive my dad. I do not blame him for what I went through as a child. My brother, sister, and I lived with my dad for two years until a traumatic event caused my sister to leave. The night she left, she came into our bedroom to let me know that she and my mother would be at school the next day to pick me and my brother up. Just as she had said, they were there at school the next day. Mom knew that the only way to keep us safe was to send us far away, so she put us on a bus to her parents' house in Alabama.

Living with Papa and Nanny, I finally began to feel safe. I had a real home with parents who loved me without hurting me. By this time, I was in third grade, and I adored my grandparents and loved living with them. Even though my grandparents were older, they did a wonderful job of raising me. My mom lived in Georgia, and she visited us as often as she could.

At times I would stay with my mom for the summer, and one day she asked if I wanted to live with her in Georgia. I was happy living with my grandparents, but I also didn't want to hurt my mom. I told her, "I like living with Papa and Nanny, but if you want me to, I will." My mom told me that she understood and wanted me to be happy, but she also wanted me to know that she loved me and that if I wanted to live with her I could. We both agreed that letting me stay with my grandparents was the best decision that she could make.

My grandparents were not wealthy, but their home was filled with love and happiness. Throughout the tender years of elementary and middle school, they were the stability I had longed for and needed. They were kind and gentle people, but they also disciplined me in love when I needed it.

In 1976 I became friends with a girl named Teresa, who attended another high school in the area. She and I began hanging out on the weekends. One Friday after school Teresa asked me to go bowling with her. Before she and her parents picked me up, my grandmother told me, "Don't leave the bowling alley for any reason; stay there until Teresa's parents pick you two up."

When her parents dropped us off, we went inside and picked out bowling shoes and then chose a lane to start a game. Only a few minutes into the game Teresa started talking and flirting with one of the guys in the next lane. She came over to me and said, "Hey, they want us to go riding with them." I immediately said, "No, I can't do that; my grandmother told me not to leave the bowling alley, and if I did, I would get in trouble." Teresa kept pressing the issue saying, "Come on, no one will ever know about it." I began feeling pressured because I didn't want to spoil everything for her, but at the same time, I was torn by what my grandmother said because I didn't want to disappoint her either. I finally gave in and made the choice to go with her and the guys. Honestly, I couldn't believe that we were leaving with two total strangers, especially after the warning from my grandmother.

A few miles down the road, Teresa told me that one of the guys, Tommy, had to pick up his truck, so I needed to ride with Chris back to the bowling alley. I was uncomfortable with the whole situation and felt as though I didn't have a choice in the matter. I told her, "No, I don't want to. I want to go with you." She became upset and said, "You'll be OK. He will take you back." So, I said, "OK, fine!" *But* I wasn't fine that night, and I would not be fine for a long time after that.

The worst nightmare of my life began that night. As Tommy and Teresa pulled away in his truck, leaving me with Chris, I suddenly noticed the smug look on his face. Then, without warning, he kissed me. I didn't resist at first, but then he began to touch me. I told him, "Stop, I want to go back to the bowling alley." What he said next still sends chills up my spine. He said, "Don't worry, sweetheart. Everything will be good, and I'll take you back as soon as I am finished." I thought, *Finished with what?*

Immediately, he grabbed me and started kissing me even harder. I tried to fight, but he was too strong. I started crying and kept saying, "No, please stop!" But he pulled me into him and raped me, right there in the front seat of his truck. After he was finished, he drove back toward the bowling alley and let me out of the truck about a block away. As I was rushing to get out of the truck, he said, "You aren't going to breathe a word of this because no one will believe you." With his voice full of sarcasm, he said, "Besides, you will be in big trouble. Remember your grandmother told you not to leave the bowling alley. If she finds out, you're going to be the one in trouble, not me."

I felt like a limp rag doll just thrown in the trash. I began walking as fast as I could, crying and thinking, "How stupid of me! Why didn't I just listen to my grandmother?" That night my innocence was snatched from me. I finally made it back to the bowling alley. As I walked in the door, I spotted Teresa and Tommy. I tried to hide my tears. When Teresa saw I was crying, she said, "What's your problem?" I ran into the bathroom, and Teresa came after me. At that moment I felt as if I couldn't breathe. Then with a weak voice I cried out, "He raped me!" She said, "No, he didn't! You know you are lying. Call it what it is! Sex between two people." I was shocked! If my own friend doesn't believe me, I thought, *What's the use?* This is exactly what Chris had said would happen; no one is going to believe me. By the time I regained my composure, Teresa's parents had arrived to pick us up. Teresa angrily whispered in my ear, "You'd better not breathe a word to my parents."

On the ride home, I didn't say a word. In fact, Teresa's mother even said, "Donna, are you tired or something? You're not talking very much." I replied in a soft voice, "Yes, ma'am." I felt dirty and ashamed. I couldn't wait to get home to take a shower.

When we pulled up to my grandparents' house, I couldn't get out of the car quick enough. As I went in the door, my grandmother said, "Good. You made it home before your curfew. I don't mind you going with Teresa and her parents; she seems like a nice girl." I looked at her with a look of disgust and said, "Sure!" Then I told her, "I'm going to take a shower before I go to bed." My voice cracked as I said, "Goodnight, Nanny. I love you." Nanny said, "Goodnight, I love you too."

I couldn't get into the shower quick enough. I scrubbed as hard as I could. All I wanted was to get his horrible smell off me, but no matter how hard I scrubbed, it lingered. I still felt filthy. Then I fell against the shower wall and sobbed for what seemed like hours. Thoughts kept rolling through my mind, *It's all my fault. Why didn't*

I just listen to my grandmother and stay where I was told to? I got out of the shower and walked into my room. As I crawled into bed, I buried my head in the pillow and wept all night. That night, out of the fear of what it would do to my grandparents and of losing my friend, I decided to keep what had happened a secret. No one would have to know. That was the moment I made the choice to live in denial. I tried to keep everything as normal as possible, but I couldn't. My grades began to drop, and I just didn't care. I wanted to move on and block everything that happened that night from my mind, but soon I would find out that the unexpected had happened, sending me over the edge.

Although I don't remember many details about the time after the rape, somehow my mom showed up and took me to see a doctor. I have no memory of the doctor telling me that I was pregnant. As I am writing this, it's almost like watching a movie, and then suddenly, the screen goes black. I had blocked everything out because I just couldn't face the truth. I remember walking out of the doctor's office and my mom giving me a look of disgust, and her harsh words telling me, "I ought to just leave and never turn back." This only added to the depth of my hurt. At that time, my mom had no idea what had happened to me. All she knew was that her sixteen-year-old baby girl was pregnant. I chose to keep silent and not tell her or anyone else that I had been raped. Thoughts ran rampant in my head, *What if I hadn't left the bowling alley with two strangers and my friend? Why didn't I* stand up and say, *"No, I'm not going?"* My heart ached as I walked toward my mom's car, and we drove off in silence.

No doubt my mom struggled to know what to do. Ultimately, she made the choice to take me to a Planned Parenthood clinic in Birmingham, Alabama. The day that she took me was surreal. Even the hour-long drive seemed like a dream. When we arrived at the clinic, I was checked in and prepped for what they called "the procedure." The procedure was a saline abortion.

The details of a saline abortion are diabolical. The saline solution is injected directly into the womb through the abdomen which then goes into the amniotic fluid. The baby drinks the solution, and like fire, the poison burns the baby from the inside out. This was 1976, during that time it was not common to have ultrasounds. The nurses at the clinic kept telling us, "It's just a blob of tissue." I shudder to think what my precious little baby must have felt, enduring such horrible agony and pain. I still cry to this day.

After the injection, we had to go back to our hotel to wait. Confused and unsure of what was happening, I felt something strange in my stomach. Young and naïve, I began feeling movements in my abdomen, but I had no idea what was going on inside of me. Suddenly I began feeling extreme pain. I had no idea that it was contractions. We went to the Baptist Medical Center Hospital in Birmingham, Alabama, next to the Planned Parenthood Clinic. I went into full-blown labor and delivered a baby, not a blob of tissue. The nurse made a huge mistake. After I had given birth, she forgot to close the curtain around the bed. As I looked to the right, I could see a large jar with what looked like a baby. I knew it was my baby.

I screamed at the top of my lungs, "I want my baby, I want my baby!" Nurses, doctors, and interns were all running over to me to see what was happening. One by one they tried to quiet me. One was saying, "Hush, hush, hush, everything is going to be fine." Another was saying, "Stop making all that noise!" The doctor, with a stern look on his face and a sharp tone in his voice, said to the nurse, "Pull that curtain right now!" But that didn't help. I had already seen the jar. With ear-piercing screams, I was still pleading for them to give me my baby. The nurse came into the area, closed the curtain, and got right into my face and said, "Shut up! You'll be just fine." I kept sobbing and screaming until finally everything went black. They must have given me something to knock me out, because the next thing I remember was waking up in the back seat of my mom's car.

In total disbelief, I questioned, "What just happened?" I thought, *This must be a nightmare. Please, someone wake me up.* At home I shut myself up in my bedroom, secluded and not wanting to talk with anyone. A hatred for everyone began to stir inside me, but especially for those involved: the doctors, nurses, my mother, and even my sister, although she was just there for moral support.

My life would never be the same. From that moment on I had no feelings for anything. I was numb and spiraling out of control. I went into a full-blown depression, and constant suicidal thoughts plagued my mind. I was so absorbed with those thoughts that I began acting on them. I had countless nightmares of screaming babies drowning in their own blood as I tried to save them. It made sleep something that I would rather avoid. The nightmares seemed so real. Later I learned that those nightmares were exactly what my baby went through because of the saline solution. I continued through life loathing people in general, but there was an extra hatred for those involved in such lies and deceit. I hated myself the most for not fighting for my precious little baby. I began to think that I didn't deserve to have a happy life, much less to live.

In 1978 I graduated high school, which was a miracle, and I moved to Georgia to be with my mom. The nightmares continued to plague me. However, I continued to hide the pain behind the mask of denial and shame.

In 1984 I met a young lady named Donna, who had just moved back to Georgia from Texas. She had family living in my area. Two of her brothers came to visit one weekend, and we all decided to go to the movies. Rick, her second oldest brother, and I decided to separate from them and go our own way. Things got out of hand for both of us, and we ended up going too far. I still believed that I did not deserve to be happy. I was twenty-five at the time, and it's sad, but Rick was just another person that would come and go; we meant nothing to each other.

A couple weeks after Rick's visit, I moved with my job to Orlando, Florida, which was about thirty minutes from where he lived. We periodically saw each other.

My roommate started noticing that I was acting a little strange, and she asked me what was wrong. I told her, "I think I might be pregnant." My next thought was, *Oh, dear God, no!* My roommate said, "Just go to the clinic up the street here and have a pregnancy test done."

The next day my roommate and I went to the clinic. The results came back; I was pregnant. I began crying and saying, "What am I going to do?" My roommate said, "Well, you need to tell Rick." It was a couple of days before I could get up the nerve to call him. The day that I finally called, he answered the phone.

"Hey, Rick, I really need to see you and talk with you about something."

"Well, I can't talk right now. Just tell me what it is about."

"I can't tell you over the phone."

In a harsh tone, he said, "Just tell me!"

I blurted out, "I'm pregnant."

Rick responded, "I don't care. Do whatever you have to. Get rid of it!" and he hung up.

I cried all night thinking about what I was going to do. At that time things weren't looking good at my job, and my roommate decided to move out. So here I was, stuck with the full load of rent, and I had no idea how I was going to make it. I made the decision to move back to Georgia with my mom again. My thought was to get a job and start over. But now I was faced with another crisis pregnancy.

I had not planned on telling my mom, but on the first night, while we were sitting in the dining room having a cup of coffee, she looked at me and said, "You're pregnant, aren't you?"

I almost fell out of my chair. "How did you know?"

"I just did. Mothers can pick up on these kinds of things." Then she said, "It'll be OK."

I felt comforted and thought that everything would now be OK. The next morning Mom woke me up by telling me, "Let's go shopping in Savannah." My thought at the time was that she was just trying to help me get my mind off things. We drove to Savannah and pulled into an area that looked like downtown. We got out of the car, and as I walked up to the door of the building, I noticed that it was not labeled. I opened the door and noticed the people sitting inside; they were young girls and women, only a few men. They looked very somber and pale. as if they had been crying. At that moment I knew what was happening. My first thought was, *Oh no, not again!* and I heard an audible voice inside of me say, "Run!" At the time I didn't know this was the voice of God. I did not listen to His voice, and I paid a terrible price for not speaking up and allowing myself to be coerced into this horror once again.

It became even more real to me as I was lying on the table. They turned on the suction machine, which was much like an industrial vacuum cleaner, and at that moment I realized what was happening. I heard bones cracking. Franticly I began weeping and begging them, "Turn it off, turn it off! Stop! Stop!" But it was too late. I screamed in anguish, "What have I done to my babies? What have I done to my babies?" Everything came rushing back to me: the rape and seeing my first baby in a jar. It all came crashing back like a nauseating horror movie, but it wasn't a movie. It was real. My heart ached so much that I wished that I could just bleed to death right there on that table.

I couldn't seem to get over how I could be such an appalling person to allow this to continue. The hatred became more intense and grew inside me. I despised myself and everyone around me that much more. What could I ever do to make up for what I had allowed? I tried to commit suicide but failed as God intervened in my life. I asked God, "Why don't You just let me out of this mess? I don't deserve to live. Please God, just kill me and get it over with!"

I don't think people realize what young girls go through after the choice of abortion is made. Whether it is by their own choice or by a coerced choice. The choice is final and the horror of it looms over them for years afterward. By that time, I was attending the church where Rick's father was the pastor. I began counseling with him. I talked to him about the guilt of allowing it to happen a second time, knowing what had happened before. He tried to encourage me that God would forgive me if I would just ask. I told him that I didn't deserve to be forgiven after what I had done. He responded, "You're right. You don't deserve forgiveness. None of us do. That's why Jesus went to the cross, for the sins of us all who deserve the penalty of death. Instead, He chose to pay the price for us and gave us the forgiveness we didn't deserve."

At the time, I was bound by guilt, shame, and condemnation, and I couldn't quite comprehend what he was saying. Even though I wanted God's forgiveness so badly, I didn't know how to accept it. That day I took all the secret hurts, pains, and sins, and packaged them up and buried them and didn't talk about them again for many years to come.

I subconsciously wanted another baby to replace the one that I had lost and not fought for, so I ended up getting pregnant by my boyfriend Staff. When I told him I was pregnant, he seemed happy about it. We were riding down the road, and he was smiling. I really couldn't figure out why he was smiling because it wasn't a reaction I had ever gotten before. I didn't know what to think about that, so I looked at him and asked, "What are you smiling about?" He said, "I don't know, Donna, I've just been told I am going to be a dad and that makes me happy." He then said, "Let's get married." So, we went that day to the Health Department to get blood tests and make plans to get married. Because it was late in the day, we decided to wait and talk about it more the next day. Even though I thought things were looking good for me, I just couldn't bring myself to go home and face my mom with yet another pregnancy. Instead I spent the night with my friend Kimberly. Staff went home and stayed at his parents' house. In the morning I called, and his mother answered the phone. I asked to speak with Staff, and she said, "He doesn't want to talk to you." Speechless and overwhelmed at her response, I hung up and told my friend what she said. My friend said, "You need to call back and tell her that you have to talk to him." I called a second time, and his mother answered again. She said the same thing. All my hopes were crushed. This was the beginning of another roller-coaster ride of emotions and events. I should have known this happiness wouldn't last. After all, I didn't believe that I deserved a happy life. How can this be happening to me again? What is wrong with me?

In such a state of confusion, I did not know how I was going to face my mom. I wasn't sure if I could stand up for myself and make the right choice. After some thought, I chose to go for counseling with the pastor at my church. I told him that I was pregnant and begged Bill Ligon not to tell my mom. He said, "Donna, we have to tell her." I started to panic and kept saying, "No, we can't do that. No, please don't tell her!" He said, "Donna, it will be OK. I will be with you, and we will tell her together that there are only two options: keep the baby or put the baby up for adoption." We told my mom, and to my disbelief she handled it differently than with the other two. She seemed to agree with my pastor that there were only two choices to be made and abortion was not one of them.

Some women from the church mentioned a place to me called Heritage House, Home for Unwed Mothers, on the property of PTL in Fort Mill, South Carolina. I had so many thoughts running through my head; I wasn't sure what I should do. I decided to visit my friend Donna, who lived in another neighborhood near me. When I arrived, she was leaving for the evening but said, "Why don't you stay here and gather your thoughts. Think about how you are going to handle all that is going on in your life." I was left all alone to deal with the chaos that I had gotten myself into. I began to cry. My life was in such turmoil, and I didn't know what I was going to do. I cried out to God, "Look at this ugly mess I've made of my life. Just look at it! What am I going to do?" I started to cry even harder, "God, can You do anything with this mess I've made?" Suddenly, I heard a voice inside me say, "Turn on the TV." I thought, *That's silly, absolutely crazy, and definitely not God.* I heard the same voice again, and I finally gave in and grabbed the remote and turned the TV on. At that moment, Tammy Faye Bakker was singing, "He'll take your mistakes and turn them into a miracle." Again, I burst into tears, fell on my knees, and prayed, "God, can You really take this mess that I've made and turn it around?" Suddenly I began to feel a peace I had never felt before. I knew exactly what I needed to do. The thought of the place that the ladies at church had mentioned suddenly came to my mind. Deep down I knew this was someplace that could help me.

My friend returned from her dinner date, and I instantly said to her, "I have to go home and talk with my mother. I need to let her know what I am going to do." On the way back to my mom's house, I began to think and play out the scenarios in my mind. I thought, *OK God, if You really want me to go to this girls' home, I need confirmation, and let it come through my mom.* When I arrived home, I knew I had to talk to my mom right away or I would talk myself out of it. So I said, "Mom, I need to talk to you about what I need to do with my life. If I am going to stay here, I need to get my priorities in order. I need to get a job and get my finances in order." Mom said, "Wait a minute, I'd like to show you something that came in the mail today from the Heritage House, Home for Unwed Mothers." As I looked at the contents of the packet, my mom said, "Donna, I feel that this would be really good for you, and you wouldn't have to deal with me or anyone else trying to sway your decision. You could have time to pray and seek God about what to do." At that moment I knew it would be the best thing for me.

I lived at the home for the first five months of my pregnancy. Finally, I had made a choice to surrender everything in my life, including the decision of this pregnancy, over to God. I knew that it would take a miracle from Him to turn my life around, and I could not do it on my own. I began reading Scripture out loud to my baby. Somehow I knew that my baby heard everything I said.

One weekend I was granted a free pass to have visitors, and my mom came to visit me. I was still praying for the best decision for me and the baby. I knew deep down in my heart what I wanted, but I never said a word. During her visit, I tried talking to her about the baby; I even mentioned a few names that I liked. But my mom didn't respond like I wanted her to. It really upset me and made me sad. I wanted to go through this pregnancy happy with the decisions I was making, but I wanted my mom to be happy as well. She left, and I continued to pray, seek God, and receive counseling to make the best choice I could for my baby.

One day a group of us went to a concert with Cheryl Ingram, who at the time sang with Kenneth Copeland's ministry. In the middle of a song, she stopped singing. She pointed over to the front row where I was sitting and said to me, "There's a child in your womb, created in the love of Jesus. Anointed is he to do the works that I have called him to do." At that moment, I began to cry. I had no idea that God even knew my name, much less cared about what was going on with me. This was the beginning of me learning that God was real and that He loved me more than I could ever imagine. He wanted a real relationship with me. Cheryl talked with me after the concert and said, "I don't know if you've been told what you are having, a boy or a girl, but I feel that I should tell you that it's a boy." I knew the moment she said it that I was having a boy.

Even after this, I was still confused about my choice of adoption or keeping the baby. Each time I attended my counseling sessions, my counselor would ask me the big question, "Have you made a decision yet?" She let me know she wasn't trying to push me into anything, she just wanted to give me the opportunity to decide without being coerced. One day I went back to my room after my session, and I laid on the floor and began praying. I had never thought to ask God what He wanted me to do. I cried out to Him, "God, what do You want me to do?" Though thoughts of keeping the baby were in the back of my mind and in my heart, at that moment I surrendered everything to Him. All I wanted was to make the right choice for me and my baby. I needed to make the decision I felt God wanted me to make. This was a first for me. After all, I had not been allowed to make any choices in my life previously. Then at that moment I had a vision. I saw myself holding a baby and walking up to Jesus and giving the baby to Him. I thought, *Well I guess this means the answer is to put my baby boy up for adoption.*

A couple weeks after I had the vision, I finally had a weekend free from work, and I thought that I would take a bus home to visit my mom. As the time for me to leave came closer, I had a strong sense that I needed to take all my belongings with me. I felt that I would not be returning. I didn't understand why because I knew how my mom felt, and the vision that I had was of me giving my baby to Jesus. Since I didn't have a lot of things with me anyway, I took it all with me. I had no idea what was in store for me.

When I arrived, Mom and I talked a little before we went to bed. The next morning she decided that she wanted to go out and get some breakfast. She said, "But first let's go by the furniture store up the street here. I want to show you something." I thought she wanted to show me some piece of furniture she had found for herself. As we were looking around the store, she suddenly said, "Come back here, Donna. I want to show you something." As I got closer to her, I could see that she was standing next to a baby crib. She then asked me, "What do you think of this?" pointing to the crib. I wasn't sure if it was a trick question or not, because at one time she could not bring herself to talk about the baby much less talk about a crib. What my mom said next changed everything and touched my heart in such a beautiful way. She said, "Donna, God has told me to do whatever I have to do to help you raise this baby you are carrying." I broke down right there in the store, bawling, not knowing how to handle all that was happening to me. The goodness of God was so much more than I could comprehend. We hugged in the store that day, and my mom said, "Donna, I'm so sorry for all that I've done that has caused you so much hurt." At that moment God showed me that in my vision I was just like Abraham who was willing to sacrifice his only son. I was willing to surrender my baby to Him, and He in return, handed my precious little baby boy back to me and entrusted me to take care of him. We still went to breakfast together, and this was the beginning of God restoring our relationship.

On Friday, December 13, 1985, my birthday, I fell off the front steps of my mother's porch. It was only three steps down, but I felt like such a klutz, pregnant and falling down steps. I could not get up at first, so I just sat there in the front yard on the walkway while cars were passing by. I thought, *Oh, I am sure this is such a pretty sight.* I wasn't in any pain or anything; I was just a little embarrassed. I finally got up, went inside, and continued about my day. On Sunday, I noticed that I was leaking a little. Honestly, I thought it was just the baby sitting on my bladder. I had an appointment at the doctor the next day, so I decided to wait until then to discuss the fall. I wasn't due until December 31, but I had scheduled weekly appointments. On Monday, December 16, I went to my appointment and told the doctor what had happened. He examined me and left the room. When he came back in, he said, "Donna, this is serious. This is not your bladder leaking. It's the amniotic fluid leaking." He asked me how long this had been happening. I told him that I hadn't noticed anything until Sunday afternoon. His next words were stern, "Donna, I want you to go straight to the hospital right now. This is very serious This could kill the baby." Panic came over me as I began to cry. I knew I needed to heed what the doctor was saying, but I also felt I needed to let my labor coach, Tammy, know what was happening and that I was going to the hospital. So first I went to the church I attended and where Tammy worked. After telling her what the doctor said, I talked to one of the pastors and asked him to pray for me. I then went straight to the hospital. It was about 3:00 p.m. when I checked into the hospital. I was put into a labor room and began the long process of giving birth. Back then they didn't have individual rooms where family could stay with you. It was just a regular hospital room on the labor and delivery floor. The nurse checked to see how much I had dilated. At the time, I was only 2 cm which wasn't good. My water had broken and too much time had passed. Things were not progressing like the doctor wanted. He said, "We may have to take the baby by C-section, but I'm going to wait it out a little longer and see what happens." They then gave me twilight anesthesia. They said with this medication I wouldn't remember the pain or anything about the delivery. Well, not with me. I remembered everything that happened. The doctor came in, checked me, and finally, to the glory of God, I was dilated to seven centimeters. They took me to the delivery room where I began to deliver my baby boy. I remember the doctor telling me to stop breathing and push. I remember thinking, *If I stop breathing, I'm going to die.* I could see that the doctor wasn't happy with me as I was still trying to figure out this "stop breathing and push thing." So, the doctor yelled, "Just stop breathing and push!" I cried to the nurse, "Do what?" My mind was just not comprehending what they were asking me to do. As I look back on this,

I'm sure the drug had something to do with my confusion. Finally, thirty-two hours later I gave birth to a baby boy, six pounds eleven ounces, nineteen inches long at 11:45 p.m. on December 17, 1985.

My son was immediately taken away from me, and I remember thinking, *Where is my baby?* Later I realized that all along he was right there in the room with me. Not long after I delivered, I started feeling like something was swelling in the back of my throat. It felt almost like huge blood clot. I kept trying to tell the nurse that something was in the back of my throat. I was trying to say blood clot, but the words wouldn't come out correctly. Suddenly I felt as if the breath was being squeezed out of me, and I blacked out. I learned later from my doctor that I had an allergic reaction to the drug that was used to bring me out of twilight. My mom was in the waiting room with some of my friends. As soon as the doctor arrived, she asked, "How is the baby?" The doctor told her, "The baby is fine, but we almost lost your daughter." My mom asked what happened, and he told her that the drug caused my uvula in the back of my throat to swell and caused me to stop breathing. I ended up having to stay in one of the labor rooms and be monitored throughout the night before being taken to a room the next day on the floor of the nursey.

I named my little boy Matthew Aaron. Matthew means "gift of the Lord." That is exactly what God gave me. He gave back to me the baby boy that I handed to Him in the vision. He entrusted Matthew to me to take care of.

Entrance to Healing

Eight years later, I was at church one Sunday morning, and a young man named Patrick, director of the Care Net Center in my hometown, was speaking. He mentioned an eight-week counseling group called "Forgiven and Set Free Post-Abortion Study." Before I knew it, I was standing in front of him and his wife, Natalie, crying my eyes out. I told them that I'd had two abortions, and I felt I needed this.

In March of that year, my sister, Sherry, suddenly died from a heart condition at the young age of thirty-seven. We were close, and her death was a shock to us all. Though still grieving, I went ahead and attended the course at Care Net, but my grief prevented me from being able to get the full benefit of the classes. However, one good thing came out of this course; I received the names of my babies. At the end of the last session, each woman prayed and asked God if her aborted baby was a boy or a girl. If the woman had multiple abortions, she would ask for each one. I prayed and felt very strongly that God showed me that my first baby was a little girl. I prayed for a name for her, and God gave me Christian Nicole. He let me know that the second baby was a boy, and He gave me Richard David. We then had a memorial service for our babies and were given a flower for each baby. At the end, I mentally took my babies and my story, with all the good, bad, and ugly things, and buried them all, never to be remembered or talked about again. My thoughts were, *I've done this. Now I don't ever need to talk about it again. No one needs to hear anything about this, ever.*

Seventeen years later I was living what I thought was a normal life. God had blessed me so much. I had come so far from the scared and insecure young girl who was afraid of everything and everyone. God had brought me through so much. In 2010 He started dealing with me about talking to Rick, the father of my second baby, and what I had allowed to happen. At the time I argued with God because I had no reason to ever talk to him again. After all it was his choice to tell me that he didn't care about the pregnancy and to do whatever I had to do to get rid of it. To me, talking to him about this was totally out of the question.

Through the years Rick and I had maintained a business relationship. We were still friends, and his sister and I were still good friends. Rick, who was now living in Orlando, and I talked about business but never about our time together at all. I wasn't about to open my heart up to him concerning it. I thought, *I am fine just like I am.* God told me, "This is not about you. It's about him." I replied, "Well, You are a big enough God. If he needs healing, You surely don't need me."

Rick came into town November 2010 and left a message asking if I would like to have coffee with him. I called him back and told him, "I can't make it, but my friend wants to come to Orlando soon." She wanted to visit one of the theme parks, and I knew we might take a trip there. He said, "When you do, give me a call. I'd like to get together and talk. I understand you have something you want to talk to me about." His sister had told him that I wanted to talk to him sometime, but she didn't tell him what it was about.

A month passed and I felt I was supposed to do a three-day water fast. I hadn't fasted a lot, but once I committed to this fast, it was the easiest one that I had ever done. By the end of the third day, I broke down and said, "God, whatever You want me to do, I'm willing." So I called my friend and asked her if she still wanted to go to Orlando. She said yes, and we made plans to go that weekend.

When we arrived, I called Rick to make plans. He said, "I know you are wanting to talk to me. We can go to dinner tomorrow night." He asked if I wanted to meet him by myself or have my friend come along too. I told him that I wanted my friend to join us.

The next day the time came for us to meet at the restaurant. On the way I was having an internal conversation with God. "Now this was Your idea, so I'm not going to be the one to bring this up. He will have to be the one to do that." At the restaurant, we enjoyed our dinner and conversation, and all the while I was thinking, *I wonder how this is going to happen?* I knew that he probably wasn't going to say anything with my friend there, and I surely wasn't going to say anything. Almost on cue, my friend excused herself to go to the restroom. The next thing I know, Rick leaned across the table and said, "About what happened with us years ago," to that I replied, "You mean twenty-six years ago?"

Rick looked at me strangely as if to say, "You've kept up with the time?"

He then said, "Yeah, I guess I just want you to know that I never meant to mislead you in any way. We were both young. I was very selfish and wanted it all my way. It didn't matter who I hurt. I don't look at you that way anymore."

"Rick, you do know that I was pregnant, don't you?"

"Oh yes, with Matthew after us."

"No, Rick, I was pregnant with your baby."

"Why didn't you tell me, Donna?"

"Rick, I did. I called you."

Almost in unbelief he replied, "What did you say to me?"

"I told you I was pregnant."

He looked shocked and said, "What did I say to you?"

"Rick, you said these exact words: 'I don't care. Do whatever you have to. Get rid of it!'"

I was surprised as Rick buried his face in his hands. Then he looked up with tears in his eyes and said, "Oh my gosh! I can hear myself saying those exact words to you." My heart broke for him as he kept saying, "What have I done to you? Twenty-six years you've handled this by yourself. What have I done to you?" Over and over he apologized, asking me to forgive him.

When my friend returned from the restroom, Rick asked her to drive my car back to the hotel so that he and I could talk more. I was able to tell him that his dad is the one who counseled me after the abortion of our baby. Rick was so overwhelmed that his dad had never said anything, but even more so that his dad still loved him even after everything that had happened.

I told him that his dad couldn't say anything to him because I told to him in confidence as a pastor, and he just acted out of the love of his heavenly Father. Then I asked Rick, "Would you like to know the name that God gave me for our son?" He answered, "Yes, I would." I told him, "God gave me the name Richard David." He immediately began to cry. I had no idea that this was Rick's full name, and he knew that there was no way that I could know it. God had this whole meeting planned out way before it happened. When He gave me the name in 1993, He knew that Rick and I would meet again, face to face, and God would heal Rick's heart and our friendship with the truth. To this day Rick is like a brother to me. After so many struggles in relationships and marriages, he is now married to a beautiful woman of God.

On the drive back home, my friend said, "I have something to confess. I had an abortion, and no one knows about it, not even my parents." She added, "I would like to go through the Forgiven and Set Free study that you did, but I don't want to go by myself." I immediately said, "I will go through it again with you, and I will be there to support you."

The next day I called Patrick, who was the Care Net Center director in our area, and his wife, Natalie, who was the leader of the Forgiven and Set Free group that I went through in 1993. I asked if I could meet with them to tell them about what had happened recently with me and the father of my second aborted baby. They agreed. I told them everything that had happened, and suddenly Patrick asked me, "Can you write that in four minutes?" To which I replied, "You mean now?" He said, "No, we are having a Right to Life rally this weekend on the doorsteps of City Hall. Would you be willing to share your testimony?" I immediately said, "Yes!" But I wanted to take back my words as soon as they'd come out of my mouth. I had never stood before a group of people and poured out my heart about anything, much less something so painful as this. My story had been buried way too long, but God was pulling me out of the grave where I had buried everything. Like Lazarus, God was calling me out of the grave of my hopelessness and despair to share the truth of what abortion does to the baby and to so many women who feel that there's no other choice. In January 2011 I shared my story at my first Right to Life rally, and I knew that God wanted to resurrect life inside me so that others would know that life matters to Him in every way, starting with the unborn.

While at church one Sunday morning a couple of weeks later, Patrick asked me if I had received his email. I said, "No, my email was down on Friday." He then said, "I am speaking this morning on the sanctity of life and would like for you to share your testimony, if you would like to?" I was thinking, *Let me look in my purse for my bullet point notes that I had used when I shared my story at the City Hall.* I began searching for my notes, but I couldn't find them. Fear came rushing over me. *This is where everyone knows me, and this is something about me that no one knows.* I had shared it with only a few people, and now everyone would know my secret. My mother was there, and I didn't want to hurt her. I'm sure I looked confused and troubled. Patrick told me, "You don't have to do this now, if you feel like you can't." He then said, "Donna, there will be other opportunities to share, God is going to open big doors for you."

Battling the thoughts of what it might do to my mother and not being able to find my notes, I declined the opportunity to speak. Patrick walked away, and then unexpectedly, I grabbed the hands of the lady sitting next to me, and I said to her, "You need to pray for me." She began to pray as if I was going to share my testimony, "As she gets up to share, I ask you Lord, give her the words to say." And while she was praying, I heard these words inside of me, "If you will open your mouth, I will fill it."

Then the woman said, "The Lord says, 'If you will open your mouth, He will fill it.'" Abruptly, I jumped up and ran down the aisle to tell Patrick. "God says I have to do it." He said, "OK, but you don't have to use any names." I said, "OK."

That morning I told my story for the second time. I shared how the blood of Jesus brought redemption to my traumatized life. That day God showed me that my life was as Revelation 12:11 says, *"They overcame and conquered him because of the blood of the Lamb and because of the word of their testimony"* (AMP). We overcome by the blood of the Lamb, and we bring the redemptive blood of Jesus into the lives of others when we share our story.

Two days later, my mom and I were in the car together, and she looked at me and said, "Donna, I want you to know that I am so sorry. Please forgive me. I never meant to hurt you. I never meant for you to go through all the pain and suffering that you did. I never knew. I was naïve until I watched a live medical show of an abortion being performed. A light came on inside me. I knew that I had believed the deception of the enemy about this."

I said, "Mom, I forgave you a long time ago, but thank you for talking with me and supporting me in what God has called me to do, to share the truth with everyone I can."

For years I have prayed, "Lord, could You just give me a dream about my babies, a vision or something, anything to let me know they are OK?" About a week after I shared my story, I attended a small group worship time with friends. While I was sitting on a white couch, worshipping God with my eyes closed, I was suddenly translated to heaven. I was no longer sitting on the couch. I was sitting on the most beautiful park bench I had ever seen in my life. There was nothing on earth that could compare. The wood was the finest I had ever seen, and I noticed a beautiful gold trim on it. As I was looking at the park bench trying to figure out what was happening, a little girl and a little boy came running up to me. I instantly knew they were my children. They jumped in my lap and started kissing me, my son on one cheek and my daughter the other. In the sweetest voices I have ever heard, they kept saying, "We forgive you, Mommy. We forgive you, Mommy. We love you, Mommy. We love you." The last thing they said was, "We'll see you again!" Instantly, I was sitting on the white couch again. I was overcome with such joy. God had allowed me to see my two children in heaven. I had grieved so much for them, and I had prayed for so long that somehow He would let me know that they were good. He answered my prayer.

From that moment I knew that I could never keep my story buried because God resurrected it. He wants it to be shared so that others can know that His forgiveness is real. He wants you to know how much you mean to Him and that nothing is too hard for Him. You haven't gone too far for His love to reach you. All you need to do is call out to Him and He will answer you. I love what Jeremiah 33:3 says, *"Call to Me, and I will answer you, and show you great and mighty things, which you do not know".* And what Jeremiah 29:11 says in *The Message* translation, *"I know what I'm doing. I have it all planned out—plans to take care of you, not abandon you, plans to give you the future you hope for."*

The enemy wants nothing more than to keep us in bondage to our past. But Jesus wants us to know that His blood has cleansed us and healed us from our hurts and pain. He wants us to know that nothing in our past is ever wasted. Even the most horrible, painful things in our lives can be used to bring hope, healing, and life to those today who need it.

> *As for you, you meant evil against me, but God meant it for good in order to bring about this present outcome, that many people would be kept alive [as they are this day]* (Genesis 50:20 AMP).

I would encourage any young woman who has been through anything tragic such as rape, abortion, or any kind of abuse to not keep it buried. Allow God to come into that place and heal every hurt and wound you have.

> *He heals the brokenhearted and binds up their wounds* (Psalm 147:3).

During the time of writing my story, the Lord gave me a poem to remind me that my voice counts and is very much needed, but it's not only my voice that counts— yours does too. Someone needs to hear your story, someone needs to hear how God brought you through and if He can do it for me, He can and will do it for anyone else. Will you make your voice count?

Your Voice Counts

Your voice can give strength to the weak.

Your voice can soothe and comfort the hurting and the broken.

Your voice can change, even the hardest of hearts.

Your voice can even shatter the strongholds that have held many in bondage.

Your voice to those on the brink of death, is LIFE.

Don't be silent! Your voice counts.

Healing Comes

While writing my story, I realized I had dealt with the pain of the abortions and received forgiveness, but this wasn't the case with the rape. Tina, one of our producers at the time, was helping me write my story. I started to talk about it, but I got angry and started crying. I told her, "I can't do this. I am not even sure God wants me to do this." Then I went back to my office. But she came to me and said, "Donna, God is going to take this from you. Trust Him." Those words rang though me to the core. I so wanted to believe them, but I still was strug-gling at that time.

On October 26, 2017, Jesse Duplantis was a guest on Sid Roth's *It's Supernatural!*, where I am employed. At the end of the program, Jesse gave a prophetic word to the television audience. At the time, I was sitting on the side with a couple of the other guest's family. Jesse pro-ceeded to say:

> You want a visitation, it's going to come. Don't do what I did and say, "Oh no, Jesus." Receive that. Let me tell you what's going to happen. The body is going to do this (shake). The body can't handle anything spiritual whether it's a devil or an angel....It's a natural thing, but it'll calm itself down, and then you just listen to what God has to say to you. You're going to be surprised; He is going to take away that incident that happened in that pickup truck, when you had that red blouse on. He's com-ing to take that personally away from you. That's all we're allowed to say about that, but you've got a visitation coming. Get ready. I just asked the Lord..., "When are You going to do it?" He just told me, "That ain't none of your business."...But it's soon, and that thing that happened will be washed away. You will never remember anymore. Thank You, Lord. And the only one that can do that, He has

to do it personally because you won't believe it unless He does it. So He's granted you a visitation.[1]

What Jesse didn't know was that when I was raped in that truck, I was wearing a red blouse. I was shaken up, but I tried to gather my composure so I could finish what I needed to do. I take care of the guests while they are with us. So I knew I needed to make sure they were escorted to the car and then I would be OK. As we went back toward the dressing room area, Tina, who was floor directing at that time, put her hand on my shoulders and said, "Donna, that was you." I turned away from her to hide my tears.

I said, "Tina, please don't say anything, I have to do my job." I knew if I went there, I would lose it. At that time Jesse had already headed out to the car, and Cathy, his wife, came out and put her arms around me and was just thanking me for taking good care of them. At that moment, I broke and said, "Cathy, that was me. The word that Jesse gave was me. I was raped in a truck, and I had on a red blouse. Cathy called Jesse back, and I told him what had happened. They prayed with me, and Jesse assured me that God was going to give me a visitation.

This visitation didn't come until a week later when I pulled out my computer to work on writing my story. I had written my story up until the rape but could never get through it. As I began to think about writing, I was cringing on the inside, and anger began to rise within me. My body began to shake as the tears flowed heavily upon my laptop. I grabbed a pillow and laid my head down; I sobbed harder and harder. Suddenly, the Lord took me in a vision back to where the guy had dropped me off. It was as if I was watching a television show of the whole scene. I could see myself as I fell out of the truck and was trying to get up. I could feel every bit of pain and agony I felt that day. I saw what I instantly knew was the heavenly Father gathering me up in His arms and pulling me close to Him. Close enough that I could hear His heartbeat. He stood and held me for hours while I released the pent-up anger and emotions that had been trapped inside me for forty-three long years.

After hours and hours of being in the Father's arms, I must have fallen asleep. I woke up with my computer on the side of my bed; I still don't know how it got there. I felt like a million bucks. The weight of the world had been lifted off me. As I began getting ready for work, a song started bubbling up inside me, and I began singing, "This peace the world didn't give it to me, and the world can't take it away. This joy the world didn't give it to me, and the world can't take it away." I knew this was the visitation Jesse Duplantis had spoken about.

When I got to work, I went right straight to Tina's office. Right away she said, "What's going on with you? You look different. You've had an encounter with the Lord, haven't you?"

I said, "Yes, I have." And I was able to tell her the whole story without the anger, hurt, and pain.

She said, "Donna, I could tell when you walked in my office; the countenance on your face has entirely changed. And when you told your story, you did it with no anger. You didn't run away and say, 'I can't do this.'"

I know that if God can do this for me, He can do the same for others.

Note

1. "Jesse Duplantis LIVE with Sid Roth," Sid Roth's *It's Supernatural!*, October 26, 2017, YouTube video, https://www.youtube.com/watch?feature=share&v =9ziiWEl1nFM &app=desktop.

Chapter 2

A COURAGEOUS CHOICE

COURAGEOUS IS WHAT COMES TO MIND WHEN I think of women who choose adoption. When faced with a crisis pregnancy situation, adoption is certainly not for the weak at heart. Making the decision to give the baby you are carrying up can be one of the most selfless acts one could ever do.

There are so many amazing young women who have stood up and have not taken the "easy" way out of a crisis pregnancy. What the world classifies as a problem is, in fact, an innocent baby. To call a baby a problem and use abortion as the only solution is absurd and cowardly. Yet on the other side of adoption, there are couples faced with the reality that they are unable to have biological children. Heartbroken and devastated, they cry out and pray to God for answers. Sometimes the answers come through young women like Jackie who choose to be brave and give the gift of life, not only to her baby, but also to a family who adopts their child.

At nineteen years old Jackie was a free-spirited young woman and was dating a young man named Jason. He and Jackie had known each other since they were fourteen. When his mother became terminally ill and later died, Jackie stayed by his side, comforting him, and trying to help during his difficult season. Jason was falling in love with Jackie, but she says, "I really wasn't sure about my feelings for him, I knew I liked him as a friend and enjoyed his company, but love?"

Jason bought an engagement ring and proposed. Jackie decided to take the ring, but only because she felt sorry for him; he had just lost his mom, and she didn't want to hurt him. Jackie says, "I took the ring and wore it on my right hand, not my left." She was so torn up inside, knowing she did not love him. Thoughts of marriage just didn't feel right to her, and she knew she had to end things and return the ring. When Jackie broke things off with Jason, he became extremely angry with her.

Some time passed when Jackie discovered she was pregnant. She began crying, thinking, *How can this be happening to me? Why me, God?* Confused and unsure of how things were going to play out in her life, she decided to go to a local Care Net Pregnancy Center with her mom. Not only did she receive confirmation that she was pregnant, but when they did a sonogram, Jackie learned she was having a girl. There was no doubt that she would carry this baby to term and give birth. Even with all the turmoil she was feeling inside, abortion was never an option. "I could never kill a child because I didn't feel I could care for him or her, because of my mistake. A child is not a mistake. A child is gift from God."

During the pregnancy, she began thinking about the only two choices she was willing to consider: keeping the baby or putting her up for adoption. The decision weighed heavily on her heart. She felt skeptical about adoption and wasn't sure if she could go through with it, but she was confident that God would lead her to the perfect family for her little girl. Jackie says, "I've always thought that adoption was amazing and knew one day I would have something to do with it, but never in a million years did I think I would be the one blessing a family with a special gift of a little baby girl." God has a way of taking our mistakes and creating a beautiful gift out of it. He allows us to make a choice that may be hard in that moment, but in the long run, will reap many rewards.

During Jackie's pregnancy, she reconnected with a young man named Matt, whom she had met the year before through mutual friends. They started hanging out together and became the best of friends. In the beginning, Matt didn't know about the pregnancy. When he found out, he told Jackie, "I will support you in whatever decision you make. I know God has a plan for your life." Matt was helpful and encouraging to Jackie.

On Wednesday, November 21, 2007, the day before Thanksgiving, Jackie gave birth. Even though she knew she was putting her baby girl up for adoption and that the adoptive parents had a name already picked out for her, Jackie named her Madison Nicole. She had to wait at least a day before the adoptive parents could make the trip to pick up this precious baby girl. Matt was not at the hospital when Jackie gave birth, but he arrived soon after the baby was born. He immediately fell in love with her, even though he was not the father. He told Jackie, "If you want to keep her, I will do whatever I have to and help you raise her, but I know it's your choice." Matt was becoming more and more attached to the baby. There were times that baby Madison would not eat, and Matt was the only one who could get her to drink her formula.

I am Matt's mother, and I was praying for Jackie because I knew the decision she was making was heart-wrenching. Even though it was the hardest decision of her life, she knew it was best for her little girl. It tore a hole in her heart. One night, while at a prayer group, I asked for prayer for my son's girlfriend who had just given birth to a baby girl. The pastor's wife said to me, "If at all possible, you need to get your hands on that baby girl, bless her, break off any spirit of rejection, and release her into the care of the adoptive parents."

I called Matt and asked if he thought Jackie would let me come up there, hold the baby, pray over her, and bless her. He said, "I don't know, but you can ask her yourself." He handed the phone to Jackie. She gave me permission to come and pray for baby. I went to the hospital, held her, and prayed for her. I blessed her and told her how much she was loved and wanted. I told her that she was chosen as a gift from God for her adoptive parents. I let her know that her mother loved her deeply and wanted her. As I sat there and held her, my heart went out to Jackie.

As she was going through the adoption procedures, she had looked through numerous pictures and information about couples that might be a fit. When she found the picture of the couple that she chose to raise her little girl, a peace came over her. She then noticed her favorite scripture, Jeremiah 29:11: *"For I know the thoughts that I think toward you, says the Lord, thoughts of peace and not of evil, to give you a future and a hope."* Jackie felt this confirmed that these were the right people to raise her baby.

Oh, how hard it must be to hand your baby over to complete strangers and trust God that they will take good care of her. Jackie is an example of courage. Courage is not the absence of fear or uncertainty. It is the resolve to make hard choices and follow them through.

Friday came, the day the adoptive parents would receive this bundle of joy to raise as their own. When Jackie woke up that morning, she thought, *I can't do this. I can't give my little girl to someone else. I love her too much.* At that moment she decided that she wasn't going through with it. Then the adoptive parents walked through the door of her room. She remembers: "I knew it was the right choice; it was the choice that God wanted me to make, and I could choose to not go through with it, but I had such a peace that came over me, and once again God reminded me of my favorite scripture, Jeremiah 29:11." Instantly, Jackie knew she could not go against the plan that God had for her baby girl and for her life.

Jackie says, "Honestly, I have my good and bad days, where certain things will trigger moments where I wish I would've kept her, but I know in my heart that I gave her to a family that needed her just as much as she needs them." One of Jackie's greatest desires is to meet her little girl someday.

Jackie and Matt got married on April 27, 2008, and God blessed them with a handsome little boy named Aaron on December 5, 2008. They are not only husband and wife but remain the best of friends.

Jackie's advice to anyone who is in a crisis pregnancy: "Please stop and think, but most of all pray for God to guide you to make the right choice for your baby. Know that He would have you to first choose *life*! Second, pray, and I promise He will lead you....The only sure way to know you made the right choice is that He will give you peace, even in the midst of the turmoil."

Chapter 3

BEATING THE ODDS

WHEN LYN AND KATIE MARRIED IN 2006, THEY both knew they were meant to have children. From the beginning of their marriage they started planning a family. After waiting and waiting and waiting, the months turned into years. All they had were disappointments and losses. They were willing to do just about anything to make it happen. Hormone therapies, natural remedies, and finally fertility drugs, but nothing happened. Then in 2010 Katie was diagnosed with diabetes and polycystic ovary syndrome, a hormonal disorder that can cause problems with the menstrual cycle and fertility. The gynecologist Katie was working with advised her to stop trying. Devastated at the thought of not being able to get pregnant was almost more than Katie could bear.

Lyn and Katie chose to go another route. They both agreed that adoption would be the way to go for them. It was miraculous how everything worked out and in less than ten days from starting the process they were at their baby girl's birth. Unfortunately, a day before their adoption was finalized, the biological father stepped in and requested the adoption be nullified and the baby girl be placed in his care.

This began what was one of the lengthiest and expensive court battles of their lives. Lyn and Katie were drained of every bit of strength they had, fighting to become the sole parents of this precious girl, whom they loved as if they had given birth to her. But the final court day came, and the blow of the judge's decision hit them hard. The court battle lasted five months, and in the end they lost. When the judge pronounced that parental rights would be awarded to the biological father, Lyn and Katie both felt as though the wind had been knocked out of them.

Katie says, "My forever baby left us on Father's Day 2011." As soon as the baby's dad pulled away from the house with their daughter, Lyn and Katie grabbed their packed bags and hopped in the car for a weeklong vacation; they needed to heal.

They had recently found out that they were expecting. She decided to keep a diary during the pregnancy because she wanted the baby to know how miraculous she was after all the losses and pain Lyn and Katie had gone through. The following Monday, Katie went to an appointment for a fetal scan with a maternal-fetal medicine obstetrician since she was classified as high risk and taking medication during pregnancy. This particular obstetrician was quite scary; Katie describes him as "gaunt, tall, and having a face like a gravestone." During the scan, he was motionless and did not even smile.

As the scan proceeded, it got worse. Katie wrote in her journal, as if she was talking to her baby, what she found out at that appointment: "Dr. Alexander has seen too much fluid on your neck and head. They are worried about Down syndrome, trisomy, and genetic issues. We've been asked to consider amnio and placental sampling. Each carries a risk. I had a blood test today, which will tell me our chances for issues like I mentioned. Everyone is praying for you—you are going to be just fine."

Katie was in so much pain and anguish, yet at the same time she was numb, as Dr. Alexander proceeded to tell them the probability of what could be wrong with the baby when she was born. She could face heart problems at the least and mental retardation in the extreme case. The doctor kept insisting, "To bring a child with such damage into the world is the ultimate cruelty." He counseled Katie to have an abortion, the sooner the better in his opinion. He assured them they could try to get pregnant again once Katie was healed. He had already told Katie that the baby's neural tube was so thick that it was within a few measurements of being fatal. He proposed that if they chose to continue the pregnancy, Katie would end up having a late-term miscarriage or worse a stillbirth. "And that would be a happy ending," he told them. The worst-case scenario would be delivering a baby who would be unable to survive outside the womb. Dr. Alexander claimed that the financial burden and stress of having a terminally ill baby could destroy their marriage. It was insane how much this doctor was trying to convince Katie to have an abortion.

Dr. Alexander insisted that if Katie wouldn't consider abortion at least she should do an amniocentesis and have placental sampling done, and he mentioned, "With luck it would trigger her to have a miscarriage naturally, so she would then be relieved of the guilt of choosing an abortion." The whole time he never said the word *abortion*. He used phrases such as *alternate options, terminating a nonviable pregnancy,* and *tough decisions.*

Katie left the office and called Lyn. His reaction was not what Katie expected. He didn't fly into hysterics or demand a new appointment. He immediately began praying vulnerably, "I am weary and can't take anymore loss or hurt." When Lyn arrived home, he told Katie that he was going to pray three things over their baby girl.

"Perfect healing, perfect health, and perfect life." Lyn and Katie's church group, family, and friends began praying with them during this time.

They opted to have Katie's blood tested for genetic markers despite the tremendous pressure to make a bigger decision. Katie also had a sonogram and went in for the test results. The results showed a one in three hundred fifty chance of the baby having a genetic or developmental problem. Lyn and Katie were relieved, but the doctor insisted that Katie was still considered a problem and told them once again they should terminate. She completely refused to worry. The sonogram showed no existing problems and that they were having a girl! They decided on the name Olivia, which means "peace—of the olive tree."

Katie went back to her regular obstetrician, who thought they should consider the testing recommended by the expert; her doctor wanted to make sure that at the birth, they had the right team set up at the hospital, including surgeons and grief counselors. He also did a second genetic blood test at the couple's request.

They scheduled another fetal scan. Katie said, "I was so scared I was sick, absolutely sick. I remember crying and shaking." While the nurse was prepping Katie, she kept telling her, "Everything is going to be fine."

In walked the doctor with his horribly grave face. He silently took measurements from the screen but wouldn't answer a single one of Katie's questions. After deliberating over the screen for the longest time, he asked the nurse, "Do you have the results from the blood test?" She asked him, "Which one, the one in three hundred fifty or the one in ten thousand?" At that point, his professional and detached demeanor disappeared. He snatched the paper out of her hand, while repeatedly asking, "One in ten thousand?" After reading the results over and over, he finally turned to Katie and Lyn and explained, "The blood test measured all sorts of chemicals and hormones in your blood, and the level of each present was an indicator for a potential problem." For each indicator, Katie was the polar opposite of a potential problem. In his words, Katie had the perfect pregnancy; he had never seen results like that before. At that moment he walked out and handed Katie's case over to one of his associates.

Lyn and Katie had a beautiful, healthy baby girl. Olivia is eight now and is as active as they come and full of joy, and she has even tested gifted. She's the opposite of the doctor's prediction. Lyn and Katie now have four children.

Chapter 4

KINGDOM IMPACT

IN 1956 A YOUNG, BEAUTIFUL, TIMID SEVENTEEN-year-old girl was enjoying hanging out with some of her close girlfriends. The group ended up at a place that made her feel uncomfortable. She didn't want to stay, so she asked her friends to take her home. They were having too much fun and didn't want to leave. She ended up getting a ride home with a friend she knew from school and his military buddy. The friend was dropped off first, but the driver didn't take her straight home. He forced her into the backseat of his car and raped her.

Nine months later this naïve, young woman gave birth to a precious baby girl named Jeri.

Growing up, Jeri believed she was a mistake. Her mom ended up marrying someone just so she would have a dad. That marriage gave Jeri two brothers but ended in divorce. Several years later, after living off food stamps, welfare, and social services, Jeri's mom married the perfect man...or so they thought.

Jeri's new stepdad and mom had two more sons, but things fell apart. He was an alcoholic and physically and verbally abused Jeri and her brothers. It was so intense that he would beat down their doors or crawl through glass windows to get his hands on them. One time he ran down the street after one of Jeri's brothers with a hatchet yelling, "If I catch you, boy, I'm going to kill you!" Can you imagine the fear, the pain, the hatred and bitterness Jeri must have felt?

There was only one way for Jeri to drown her feelings. When she was twelve, she began smoking and drinking. By the time she was fifteen, she was smoking weed. At sixteen she was doing and selling drugs. Her life had no meaning, no point, and no purpose. It was utterly worthless. Jeri hated her mom for getting them into their situation, and she hated her stepdad for causing so much pain. She hated her life.

When Jeri was sixteen, her family moved to Claire, Michigan. One Saturday afternoon they heard a knock on the door. A middle-aged pastor was there inviting them to church. The family politely thanked him and sent him on his way. But every Saturday for two years that pastor brought Jesus' love to her and her family's dark and broken hearts. For two years Jeri never once gave that pastor a glimmer of hope, but he never gave up; he never relented and neither did God.

Jeri was living her own way; she was doing drugs and did not care what happened to her. But God did! One afternoon, Jeri got arrested in a massive drug bust. Sitting in a jail cell all alone, she heard an audible voice, "Jeri, don't you understand? Don't you really understand? I love you."

"Mom?" Jeri cried out, puzzled and in shock. Was it her mom's voice in that jail cell? No one was around, not even another woman. It was just Jeri and God. When she got out of jail, she asked her mom if she remembered saying that. She said yes. Jeri's mother had been fasting and interceding over her, and she had cried out, "Jeri, don't you understand? Don't you really understand? I love you."

A while later Jeri was driving past a billboard with John 3:16 on it, "For I so loved you..." She knew God was pursuing her, but the thought of Him loving her caused so much fear to stir inside that it made her run from Him. She began hitchhiking and staying wherever she could. She ended up on a farm out in the country in the middle of nowhere with people she barely even knew. One night as she was sleeping, Jesus came to her in a dream. With arms stretched out and blood pouring from His hands, He said, "For you, I died." Jeri woke up, grabbed her skinny legs, and began rocking back and forth in agony crying out, "Leave me alone! I'm nothing! I'm worthless! Just leave me alone!"

Another day Jeri went home with people she met at a bar. They lived in a mobile home out in the country. No one knew where Jeri was. For the next ten days she heard silence. God didn't show up. He didn't speak in an audible voice, on billboards, or through her dreams. She began looking under tables and behind curtains just to see if God was there. That's how real He had become to her. But He was now silent. Had he finally left her alone as she had told Him to?

One afternoon she was sitting in the grungy, old mobile home alone, and she heard a knock. *What?* she thought. *Surely no one could be knocking on the door. There's no one here to visit!* Jeri got up from her chair and hesitantly yet curiously made her way to the front door. She slowly turned the knob. "Pastor?" Her heart dropped. "Wha...Wha..." She couldn't even utter a full word. The pastor immediately explained. "I was on my knees in my home, and I began crying out to God. I told Him, 'I'm not giving up on this girl. Where is she?' I got up off the floor, got into my car, and began driving out to the country to this mobile home. Here I am! I'm just as stunned as you, Jeri. I'm here to tell you that Jesus loves you and has a plan for your life!"

After the pastor left, Jeri heard the scariest words she had ever heard in her entire life: "If you don't give into Me, I'm going to give up on you." God was serious. From that moment on, Jeri would never be the same. She called the pastor's wife, and a few days later Jeri began the life-changing program Teen Challenge.

Jeri's New Life

On Monday night, October 20, 1975, Jeri Larson became a new creature. All the old things passed away, and everything in her became new! From that moment on, she began growing in the things of God. Everything around her came alive, especially His Word. She couldn't wait to wake up in the mornings and hear God's voice! He was her Father, her Restorer, her Healer, her Deliverer, her Comforter, her Everything. She fell deeply in love with Jesus, a man— something she told herself she would never do!

Somehow God seems to turn the vision we have for ourselves completely upside-down, doesn't He? Little did she know this was just the first stone He was turning over. He had a whole new adventure waiting for her just around the corner.

Jeri's life radically changed for the better! Every day was a brand-new page, and she was allowing His pen to write her story. Teen Challenge was slowly becoming the second love of her life (Jesus being the first, of course), and the wisdom she gleaned from teachers were like drops of Heaven refreshing her newly saved soul. After one year in the program, Jeri graduated and joined the team as junior staff. This was all part of her plan.

Jeri's dream was to become the first Pentecostal/ Assemblies of God nun helping pull other women out of the darkness like she had been in. Nothing in the world could take her away from this dream. She was going to stay with Teen Challenge for the rest of her life! She was about to find out she wasn't necessarily on the same page as God.

Did you guess it? That's right, stone-turning experience number two was the day Jeri realized Teen Challenge wasn't going to be in the picture for the rest of her life. David Wilkerson, the founder of Teen Challenge, had started a Bible school in Lindale, Texas. This was the last place Jeri wanted to go! She fought it and tried to convince her supervisors that she wasn't a good fit for the school. But how many times does God continue to show that His ways are higher than our ways? Nine months after being on staff, Jeri boarded her first-ever flight and stepped foot on Texan soil. She began attending Twin Oaks Leadership Academy. Boy, did she not realize the extravagant plans God had for her in this next chapter of her life.

Over the next six months Jeri's focus was on one thing only—God. David Wilkerson had chosen twenty-five men and twenty-five women Teen Challenge graduates from all over the country to attend his school for free. Jeri was determined to utilize every opportunity possible, and she began growing exponentially, but so did something else inside of her.

You see, Steve Hill was in her class. Remember Jeri's dream of being a nun? Well in her mind, the enemy was using him to hinder her call of becoming a nun! For hours on end, she would rebuke the attacks of the enemy because every time she saw him, her heart would pound uncontrollably. It felt as if it were going to explode out of her chest! "This is not right," she explained to God. "Steve Hill is the enemy's plan! It's satan's plan to use a man to destroy my call!" But no matter how many hours Jeri rebuked the devil in prayer, she needed victory! But to no avail, her love for this young man continued to grow stronger, deeper, and wilder!

One afternoon Jeri was sitting in the secretary's office doing her work. Suddenly the very trap she was trying to avoid walked straight in the door and plopped down on the swiveling chair next to her. "They know about us!" Steve Hill joyfully proclaimed, while waving his arms in the air and spinning in the chair. "What? Are you crazy? There is no us!" Jeri snapped back at Steve, who had a mischievous smile.

Little did Jeri know that while she was "rebuking the enemy," confessing her feelings to her supervisor, and avoiding that man with her entire being, Steve Hill was thanking God for giving Jeri to him as his wife! Her plan to be the first Pentecostal/Assemblies of God nun was demolished!

God gave Jeri a phenomenal God-fearing husband. The young man that she thought was a decoy from the enemy became the best thing that ever happened to her besides salvation. God gave them an amazing, loving family with three beautiful children. He has used them as youth pastors; Sunday school teachers; and missionaries to Argentina, Costa Rica, Spain, and Russia. They were also instrumental in the Brownsville Revival, one of the largest and longest-running Pentecostal outpourings in US history. Approximately four million people from all over the world came to Brownsville Assembly of God. The Lord has used the couple to plant churches all over the world; He also led them to build a Bible school, help finish a children's home, create websites, and build ministries. Thousands upon thousands have been brought into the Kingdom of God through them!

"I have experienced the sweetness of God's ultimate purpose for my life," Jeri says. "Now that doesn't mean there weren't struggles along the way." She lost three children in childbirth and went through six years of cancer with her husband before he died in 2014; seven months later their only son died. She has also dealt with heartaches with her children, but through it all, one thing always remained: God's faithfulness to her and her family.

One day Jeri's mom told her something she will never forget, "You were the best thing that ever happened to me from a bad situation." This reminds me of Genesis 50:20, *"You intended to harm me, but God intended it for good to accomplish what is now being done, the saving of many lives"* (NIV).

In her teens, Jeri's mom had gotten saved watching a Billy Graham program on TV. Jeri says, "I think that pastor coming to our house was an answer to her prayers." Jeri's mom has been living with her for years and is one of the family's greatest blessings!

Jeri wonders, "What if my mom would have aborted me because of her fear of having a child from rape?" Not only would Jeri not exist, so would her impact in the Kingdom of God and on those in need. Because Jeri's mom faced her fears and chose life, Jeri has been blessed with two beautiful daughters, who are in the ministry with her, grandchildren, and a ministry that gets sweeter and sweeter.

"Your life is worth far more than you believe. He's waiting for you!" Jeri shares. "I'm here to tell you this: no matter what circumstances you come from, your life is more valuable to Him, and He has a plan for you. If God can use a drug-addicted child born out of rape, He can also use you, and He can surely use the child yet to be born. It's time to give God our all. And it's time to be used by Him."

Chapter 5

A FATHER'S REDEMPTION

MICHAEL GREW UP IN CHURCH, SORT OF. HE knew about God and Jesus, and he heard the Bible, but he decided it wasn't appealing to him. He thought church was more of a religious thing, so he made the choice that he didn't want any part of it. Michael got involved with the wrong crowd, and drugs and alcohol became his way of life.

As a teenager, he was in a lot of bad relationships. At eighteen, he was in a toxic, polluted relationship with a young lady. There were a lot of jealousy and trust issues, and after about five months, they decided to break up.

Some months later the girl called Michael and asked him to meet her. When they met, she said, "I'm pregnant, and I know that this is your baby." Michael was heartbroken; he loved children and dreamed of the day when he would become a father. But he didn't think it was the right time because he couldn't be responsible and his life was a mess. The news really hit Michael hard, and he didn't know what to do. She told him, "I spoke with my mother about this, and we have decided to have the abortion, but we would like you to pay for it." Paying for it was not a problem for him, but his heart sank at the thought of it. He was torn but went along with their decision to go through with the abortion.

Several months later, he was suffering with depression and suicidal thoughts. He tried everything to make himself happy: more money, drugs, and relationships. Every time he got what he thought he wanted, he was still broken and empty on the inside. He finally came to a breaking point, and said, "Jesus, if You're real like people say You are, I need You right now! Jesus, I need You to change me. Do whatever *You* have *to do!*" At that moment Michael had a supernatural encounter with God. His presence crashed in and took all the fear and disappointment from Michael's heart. God poured into him a divine love and acceptance. Michael left that room free in so many ways, but he still struggled with the baggage that plagued him from the abortion.

One Sunday Michael's sister called him and said, "I think you need to come to church." Michael responded, "You know I really don't like church!" But she convinced him to go. Michael prayed, "God, You know that I don't want to go to church, but I'll go if that's what You want. But please take at least one piece of baggage off my back that's been holding me down." Michael gave God an ultimatum. He told Him, "You know what, if You'll do that, I'll go to church all the days of my life, and I'll keep going. I'll serve You forever."

Michael went to church. It was a very large church, and the pastor really flowed in prophesy and words of knowledge. The whole service had gone by and nothing had happened. Michael thought, *Thanks, God!* and decided to go to the restroom. They were equipped with speakers so Michael could still hear everything going on in the sanctuary. He heard the pastor say, "I'm getting a word of knowledge right now. The word of knowledge is that someone in here has had an abortion and is suffering with shame because of it." Michael knew in his heart that word was for him. God was speaking through the pastor's mouth straight to Michael's heart, so he ran out of the restroom. Michael was trying to find his way back into the sanctuary, but there were multiple doors that led into the sanctuary and he couldn't find one that was unlocked. Not knowing what else to do, he ran back to the restroom and into one of the stalls. He closed the door and sat down.

Michael cried out, "Help me! Whatever You need to do, just change me." Michael says, "I began feeling His glory love; it was just like the love of God, the forgiveness of God, His presence again rushing down my back like tingles. His glory wrapped around me, and all the shame, guilt and pain left."

Michael left that room completely free of shame and guilt regarding the abortion; he knew his baby was in the hands of the Lord.

A few months later, on Father's Day, Michael was at the same church. The pastor says to everyone, "Let's have all the fathers stand up and let's give them honor." All the fathers stood, and everyone clapped. Michael didn't stand because he didn't consider himself a dad. Unexpectedly he heard the Holy Spirit whisper to him, "Happy Father's Day!" Michael broke down and fiercely wept; God took his shame away and gave Michael hope that he would be united to his baby in heaven. Michael says, "God went the extra mile; He didn't have to because I was already shame-free, yet God wanted to encourage me that I am a dad and that my child is in heaven with Him."

Three years later Michael was in Mozambique with Iris Global, and God began to teach him about medi-tation and experiencing heaven. The Lord highlighted Ephesian 2:6, *"and raised us up together, and made us sit together in the heavenly places in Christ Jesus."* We are seated with Christ right *now*, not just one day in the future. It is a present reality. So Michael spent time soaking and meditating on the Word, and the Lord showed him heaven. He walked with the Lord in heaven, and He gave him glimpses and pictures of heaven. One night Michael was in a hammock, in Mozambique, in the dirt of Africa, and he was playing some worship and was just basking in God's presence. Unexpectedly everything became silent. At that moment, God took Michael into a vision, and he was in heaven. Jesus walked up to him with a baby in His arms. Michael wasn't even thinking this was his own baby, but Jesus handed him the baby and told him, "This is your baby; he is a boy and his name is Stephen." Michael became completely undone that the Lord would love him so much that He would allow him to hold his very own son.

Several years later Michael attended Christ for the Nations Bible school, and God gave him a dream. He was with a little girl who looked to be about seven or eight years old. They were on the mission field, and she was laying hands on the sick, casting out devils, and operating in the supernatural. Michael thought, *What is going on?* This little girl was just blowing him away. In the dream, he picked her up and swung her around, smiling. At that moment he woke up, and Michael says he felt the presence of God so strong and knew in his spirit he was going to have a little girl named Selah. Michael had never even heard of Selah as a name, he knew it only from the Psalms and he did not know the meaning of it.

A few years later Michael returned to Mozambique and met a young lady named Selina. He told God, "Lord, I like her; she's passionate about You, she's called, she's here. God, I like who she is." But Michael decided to lay it all down, "If it's You, good, and if it's not You, good also." Michael completely surrendered everything to God and His will for his life. That same night, he and Selina met to sing and worship together. Out of the blue Michael turned to Selina and said, "Selah," and Selina responded: "I'm going to have a little girl named Selah one day!" Michael was completely blown away by the goodness of God and this amazing confirmation. Eventually Michael and Selina got engaged, and people prophesied about the little girl they were going to have and how she would be a part of the ministry God had called them to.

Michael and Selina were married for only a year when the Lord took them to Cambodia with Iris Global. After about six months a team from Bethel was visiting and ministering prophetically. Some on the team kept telling Michael that he was a dad. He thought it meant a spiritual dad. Then Selina had an encounter with God; she was in heaven, and a little boy ran up to her and kept staring at her with a smile on his face. Selina told Michael what happened, "I knew it was Stephen, and it was as if he wanted to tell me something." A week later they found out they were expecting. They both knew that Stephen knew about their daughter Selah and that God was bringing her into their lives as a redeeming part of their God story.

Michael says, "I love sharing this story because so many need to know that if you've messed up and are battling with shame and guilt, you can be totally free. Run to Jesus instead of away from Him. Take time to allow God to encounter you with His presence and to speak hope and healing into your suffering and shame."

Chapter 6

UNEXPECTED SURPRISE

WHEN KELLY WAS SIXTEEN, SHE CAME TO THE US from Venezuela. At eighteen she met her husband, Leo, who is from Argentina. They dated for five years and got married. They were working hard for what they thought was the American dream. They were making a good income. They bought a home and new cars, and had their first baby. Things were going well, but when their son was two, Kelly realized that her husband was having an affair. She confronted him, but he denied it, and she asked him to leave.

At this time a close friend of her husband's started calling her, offering support; they had an affair. She ended it, but soon found out she was pregnant. She didn't know what to do or who the baby's father was. A coworker suggested that she take a pill (an abortion pill); she convinced her it was only a pill. Kelly's mom also gave her the advice to take the pill and move forward.

Kelly made the appointment to get the abortion pill, took it, and went back to the abortion clinic two weeks later. She was told that she was still pregnant; they forced her to put a gas mask on and a doctor performed an abortion. She was devastated. She went home crying and was a mess; she decided that was not ever going to tell anyone. She determined to keep this horrible secret to herself.

Ten years later Kelly went to a church and took a class about breaking generational curses. The pastor prayed over her and mentioned rejection. After the class, Kelly felt the need to ask her mom if she had ever had an abortion. Her mom told her something that she had never told anyone. Her mom confessed that when she was pregnant with Kelly, she was desperate. She was in her first year of law school, working full time, had a one-year-old, and was living with her mother-in-law, and she decided that it was best to have an abortion. Kelly was the twin survivor. They forgave each other. That started a process of restoration for Kelly, and she decided that she would no longer keep silent.

She has been happily married for almost twenty years; she has three beautiful kids, and she is actively sharing her story with others to bring hope and healing and change to a nation.

Chapter 7

A SINGLE MOTHER'S PLEA

THE FOLLOWING IS THE TESTIMONY OF AN anonymous single mom of four with another on the way. Her story demonstrates God's faithfulness. He keeps His promises.

For three years I had been raising my four children alone after my marriage of abuse and emotional neglect ended. I was already struggling to make ends meet financially. We were already poor. I remember the morning I woke up early and snuck into the restroom with the pregnancy test I had purchased the day before. Positive!

At that moment I flushed with heat; my heart felt like it was caving in on me. My breaths shortened and panic came over me. I felt like disappearing. I felt as if there were a huge scarlet A in the middle of my forehead. I felt like making it all go away. Suddenly, there in that restroom where I was all alone, an audible voice said, "This baby is going to save your life."

With those words spoken so gently in my ear, I knew that it was the Holy Spirit revealing Himself to me. Instantly, my body cooled, my heart calmed, and my breath returned to me. I felt the most incredible peace fall over me, but I was still so unsure and afraid of the unknown. Would my family hate me for this? Would my friends be disappointed? How am I going to tell them? I didn't want to.

As ashamed as I am to admit it, I thought it would be so easy to make it all go away so no one would ever know. I never thought I would ever consider an abortion. I had been adamantly pro-life from a young age, but at this moment I entertained it as an option. I knew that I could hide it from the world, but I could not hide it from the One that mattered, and I could not hide it from myself. I would know, and it would kill me. The Holy Spirit's words kept resounding in my ears over and over, "This baby is going to save your life." What did that mean? Literally, figuratively, spiritually? I just continued to hear them, and they continued to bring me peace.

It was about a month before I began to feel like I could no longer hide the truth from the people around me. I knew the time was coming when I was going to have to admit my sin and confess the truth. A decision had to be made. As I knelt by my bedside and called out to my King in absolute humility, I asked Him, "Lord, if I honor You with this baby, will You please honor me?" He said, "I will."

My son is now eight years old and is the most handsome, athletic, tenderhearted, intelligent, scholarly, well-behaved, and incredibly funny young man with a heart for God that I have ever met. He is the absolute joy of my family and was just what we needed at precisely the moment we needed it most. He has been the conduit that brought us all back together to a place of healing within ourselves that we may not have otherwise achieved. He has, in fact, saved our lives.

There has never been a day that we have not had more than we needed, and we have even had quite a bit of our wants met too. In times when I felt like I didn't know how we were going to make it, money and resources flowed out of the most unforeseen places. Every bill has been paid, day care payments have been made early every week, and no need has been left unmet...by the grace of

God. He has and continues to honor us. Today as I sit here writing this letter, it is so indisputably clear to me that it was never my choice.

Chapter 8

THE HOLOCAUST THEN AND NOW

MANY TIMES WE HAVE NO IDEA WHERE OUR choices will lead us. It is impossible to see into our future and what will "Happen" because of one decision. However, hindsight is always 20/20. We can look back and see where each choice led us, and sometimes we can see how our choices impacted other lives.

Sol Pitchon owes his life to the decision of one courageous doctor. Sol's mother, Garmaine Pitchon, survived one of the most horrific times in our modern-day history, the Holocaust of the Jewish people.

She was from a wealthy, well-to-do Jewish Greek family in Thessalonica, Greece. Her father's clothing factory was made tailored suits and, ironically, uniforms for the Nazis as they came into power. Having only a sixth-grade education, she still spoke five languages, which she began learning at the age of seven.

During the years leading up to the invasion of Greece, Garmaine met people who would lead her down a path that was being set for her survival. As a young girl, Garmaine noticed that her Greek friend Yanni was never home on Sundays. She asked him where he always went. He explained that he and his family went to church, and this sparked her curiosity. She wanted to see this church. Yanni agreed to take her, but he told her to wear a cross and say that her name was Maria. She attended the Greek Orthodox Church with his family, wearing a cross that she kept and hid from her devout Jewish family.

Garmaine met the Greek mother of a German officer who taught her to speak German and explained what was coming. The lady taught her to speak well of Hitler and to know and perfectly say his name, "Heil Hitler, Hitler mein Führer." With each meeting, her new friend's heart grew heavier, as she learned more from her son about the Germans' plans to kill Jews. She warned Garmaine, "You must never say that you are Jewish!" Each time they would meet, Garmaine would work on her German, all while her family believed that they would be safe under German rule. Emotions ran high as she tried to convince her mother that the Germans' plans were evil, but there was no getting through to her. To hide her deep Jewish roots, Garmaine began to wear the cross more openly and attend church, but her mother and sisters would not go with her.

It was a cold, gray time in history. The Jews were on the brink of being taken through the most vicious, vile treatment of human beings in modern times. In 1941, the Germans invaded Greece. At first the Germans made it seem like Garmaine's mother was right, that everything would be OK. The Germans had convinced them that it was a time of war, and they simply needed to submit until the war was over. However, they were always required to wear the Star of David on the back of their clothes to identify them as Jews. This was the beginning stages of their separation from the rest of society.

Garmaine's fears became her reality. Her grandparents owned a grocery store, and while visiting her grandmother, she saw German soldiers enter the store and take whatever they wanted from the shelves. This was a common scene during that time as the Germans would help themselves to items in Jewish-owned stores without paying. Her grandmother began to speak up,

"Stop! You have to pay for that!" The people in the store stood silent, waiting to see what would happen. Then the soldier walked up to her and shot her in the head right in front of Garmaine. In the store that day, she learned to be selective with her words and hide her emotions.

Her mother sent Garmaine to stay with her aunt, Argentina. During her stay she met a German Nazi named Johann. Over the course of six months they met and talked, but she maintained that she and her family were Christian Greek Orthodox. Johann grew to think of and treat her as his daughter. Garmaine reminded him of his daughter, who had died. He warned her of all that was coming, including Auschwitz. He told her, "Take your family and leave Greece. It's the only way to save yourself and them. Everyone will be dead." He warned her of the gas chambers and the prison camps, but he also told her, "You will go to Auschwitz, but you will survive it." It was his detailed warnings that gave urgency to her fears.

Before their last meeting, Johann went the extra mile for Garmaine and her family. He prepared papers for them. On the back of Garmaine's papers, he wrote that she was his daughter and asked that she not be harmed. He instructed her to keep the papers in her boots and never take them off. He also taught her to pose as a German, in clothing, speech, and actions.

Not long after she returned home, Garmaine's mother caught her practicing the German disguise. There was no way to persuade her mother that this was the only way to save their lives. Her mother was convinced that the Germans were good people, and she felt it would betray her relatives to appear to be anything other than Jewish.

Garmaine warned her closest friends, and even at her young age, began preparing for war. She continued to wear a cross and say that she was a Christian when asked, but her family would not change. It wasn't long until the Germans came to take the Jews away to the ghetto. Johann's words were becoming a reality. They had to walk to the ghetto, where they stayed for ten days. There were about a thousand people in a small space. Her family made up almost a fourth of the population of the ghetto at that time. Every member of her family was there, except her father who had been killed.

Her mother still did not believe that the Germans could have such horrific plans for them. She believed that they would only be led away to work until the war was over, but soon that belief was proven wrong. They were herded like animals into cattle cars of trains. There was inadequate ventilation and no bathroom facilities. The guards placed a single bucket of water in the car a day. For eight days they were on the train to Auschwitz. During the trip, Garmaine's youngest sister, less than two years old, died in her mom's arms. When they arrived, she was taken away and thrown onto a truck.

Doctors chose three hundred girls for experiments, and Garmaine at the age of 16 was one of them. As the doctors walked up to her, she said, "Heil Hitler." An older doctor was taken aback by how much she reminded him of his granddaughter, who had died in the gas chamber. He quickly said, "I'm going to save your life." He told her to call him Grandpa and to speak only in German. This doctor began to call her his granddaughter that day. Initially she was suspicious of him, but when he recited a Jewish prayer in Hebrew, she was convinced that he was for real and he would help her.

That day Garmaine saw her family for the last time. Her mother and four sisters were taken to the gas chambers, and she began enduring medical experiments. When it was time for her group to be taken to the operating room, Grandpa shared with her what was going to happen. At that time, she was the first to go into surgery. Dr. Josef Mengele, the infamous "Angel of Death," placed her on the operating table. They were sterilizing the girls that day. There was no anesthesia, only a blanket to bite on to cope with the pain. It took thirty stitches to close the first incision.

Then the ground began to shake. Explosions were heard all around. The Allies were bombing the camp. As they began to get closer and closer, Dr. Mengele instructed Grandpa to finish the surgery while the Nazis ran for cover. It was at this moment that Grandpa, the Jewish doctor, Dr. Samuel, made the decision to disobey the orders that he was given. He told Garmaine that he would not remove her other ovary, but she would have to keep her cycle a secret. He only asked that she remember him when she had children.

Grandpa faked the rest of the surgeries that day, but he told the Nazis that the patients had all been sterilized. Through complications and conditions, only one girl survived, Garmaine. She lived though many other horrific events during the Holocaust, but she eventually married and made her way to the United States. Unfortunately, the Jewish doctor "Grandpa," Dr. Samuel, was executed by the Nazis, but it was because of his choice that Solomon "Sol" Samuel Pitchon is alive today.

Sol was born in Thessalonica Greece not in the United States. They didn't come to the United States until years after his birth. Between January 1933 and May 1945, the Holocaust claimed six million Jewish lives, taken without regard. It is hard to imagine the amount of all the lives lost, but since abortion was legalized in the United States in 1973, according to the Guttmacher Institute, more than sixty million lives have been taken—that's ten times greater than the Holocaust of World War II.

There are choices to be made in our lives, hard choices, just like in Garmaine's story. People could have left her uninformed, or she could have decided to simply go along with what her family was telling her. If she had decided to go with the flow, she would have died in the gas chambers with the rest of her family, but she chose to fight for life.

Garmaine's son, Sol Pitchon, has personally been a part of making decisions concerning the innocent lives of the unborn. He was a psychotherapist for years, and he began connecting the dots between some of his client's issues and needs from past abortions in their backgrounds. He also personally helped walk his daughter through the decision of choosing life for an unplanned pregnancy that she experienced at sixteen years old.

He is an example of how a single choice can affect the lives of thousands. For the past twenty-one years Sol has been the president and CEO of New Life Solutions, helping men and women make the choice for life. Sol says, "My mother survived the Holocaust of World War II, and God has me serving Him in the holocaust of abortion here in America today. The Lord has a plan, purpose, calling, and destiny for every child no matter how, when, or where they were conceived."

Chapter 9

NEVER AGAIN

ABBY JOHNSON'S CHOICE TO RESIGN FROM the largest Planned Parenthood Clinic in Bryan, Texas, didn't happen until after eight years of being a part of an industry that she never truly understood. Her driving force for working at Planned Parenthood and being pro-choice was her kindheartedness and her desire to help women and make the world a better place. Her story is not neat and tidy and doesn't come gift wrapped in easy answers. In fact, it's heart-wrenching to say the least.

Abby has been brought to the pro-choice/pro-life arena for "such a time as this." She has experienced how good intentions can be warped into poor choices. We all face choices. Sometimes what we choose may seem right at the time, but one day we come face to face with the truth. This is what happened to Abby on a September day in 2009 when she was called in to assist with an ultrasound-guided abortion. It changed the course of her life forever.

The Ultrasound

In the eight years that Abby was with Planned Parenthood, she had never been called into the exam room to help the medical team during an abortion, yet this day that would all change. She asked herself, *Why would they need me?* And thought, *Nurse practitioners are the ones who assist in abortions not the other clinic staff.* As a director of the clinic in Bryan, Texas, she was able to fill in for any position in an emergency and if absolutely necessary—except for the doctors and nurses performing medical procedures. Abby, on a few occasions had agreed to stay with a patient and hold her hand during the procedure, but only at the patient's request and if she had been the counselor who'd worked with the patient during intake and counseling. That was not the case that day with this one. Abby continued to struggle with the thought of why they needed her.

That day, the abortionist who had been at the Bryan clinic a few times prior, was visiting. He had a private abortion practice about 100 miles away. When Abby had talked to him several weeks before about the job, he explained that at his facility he did ultrasound-guided abortions. This abortion procedure has the least risk of complications for the women as this method allows the doctor to see exactly what is going on inside the uterus. There is a lesser chance of perforating the uterine wall, which is one risk of abortion. As far as she was concerned, Abby felt the more that could be done to keep women safe and healthy the better. However, she explained to the abortionist that day, that this wasn't the protocol at this clinic. He understood and said that he would follow the typical procedures, though they agreed he could be free to use ultrasound if he felt a situation warranted it. To Abby's knowledge they had never done ultrasound-guided abortions at that facility.

They did abortions only every other Saturday, and the allocated goal from the Planned Parenthood affiliate was to perform twenty-five to thirty-five procedures on those days. Their typical procedure at that clinic took about ten minutes, but an ultrasound added about five minutes and when you're trying to schedule up to thirty-five abortions in a day, those extra minutes add up.

Abby felt a moment's hesitancy outside the exam room. She had never liked entering this room during an abortion procedure and never welcomed what happened behind this door. But since everyone had to be ready, at any time, to pitch in and get the job done, Abby pushed the door open and stepped in. The patient was already sedated, still conscious but groggy as the doctor's bright light beamed down on her. She was in position with the instruments laid out neatly on tray next to the doctor and the nurse practitioner was positioning the ultrasound machine next to the operating table.

"I am going to perform an ultrasound-guided abortion on this patient. I need you to hold the ultrasound probe," the doctor explained. As Abby took the ultrasound probe in her hand and adjusted the settings on the machine, she argued with herself, *I don't want to be here. I don't want to take part in an abortion. No—wrong attitude!* She would need to psych herself up for this task. She took a deep breath and tried to tune into the music from the radio playing softly in the background. Abby told herself, *It is a good learning experience to see an ultrasound-guided abortion. Maybe this will help me when I counsel women. I'll learn firsthand about this safe procedure. Besides, it will be over in just a few minutes.*

Abby could not have imagined how the next ten minutes would shake the foundation of her values and change the course of her life. She had occasionally performed diagnostic ultrasounds for clients before. It was one of the services the clinic offered to confirm pregnancies and estimate how far along the client was. The familiarity of preparing for an ultrasound soothed Abby's restlessness at being in the exam room. Abby applied the lubricant to the patient's belly, then maneuvered the ultrasound probe until the patient's uterus was displayed on the screen and adjusted the probe's position to capture the image of the fetus. Abby had expected to see what she had seen in past ultrasounds. Depending on how far along the pregnancy was and how the fetus was turned, usually she would see a leg, or head, or some partial image of the torso, and would need to move a bit to get the best possible image. But this time was different as the image was complete and she could see the entire, perfect profile of a baby... just like her little girl Grace was at twelve weeks.

Abby was surprised, remembering her very first peek at her daughter three years before, cuddled securely inside her womb. The image now before her looked the same, only clearer, and sharper. The feature shocked her. She could easily see the profile of the head, both arms, legs and even tiny fingers and toes. Perfect. And just that quickly, the flutter of the warm memory of her daughter Grace was replaced with a surge of anxiety. Abby asked herself, *What* am *I about to see?* Her stomach tightened, and she thought to herself, *I don't want to watch what is about to happen.*

You might think that sounds odd coming from a professional woman who had been running a Planned Parenthood clinic for two years, counseling women in crisis, scheduling abortions, reviewing the clinic's monthly budget reports, and hiring and training staff. But odd or not, the simple fact is, Abby had never been interested in promoting abortions. She had come to Planned Parenthood eight years ago before believing that its purpose was primarily to prevent unwanted pregnancies and thus reducing the number of abortions. That had certainly been her goal. At that time Abby believed that Planned Parenthood saved lives—the lives of women who, without the services provided by this organization, might resort to some back-alley butcher. Every bit of this sped through her mind as she carefully held the probe in place as Abby heard the nurse say, "Thirteen weeks," after taking the measurements to determine the fetus's age.

The doctor looked at Abby and said, "OK, just hold the probe in place during the procedure so I can see what I'm doing." The cool air of the exam room left Abby feeling chilled, her eyes still glued to the image of this perfectly formed baby, she watched as a new image entered the video screen: The cannula—a cylinder/straw shaped instrument attached to the end of the suction tube had been inserted into the uterus and was nearing the baby's side. Abby described what she saw, "It looked like an invader on the screen, out of place. Wrong, it just looked wrong." Her heart began to race even faster. Time slowed. She didn't want to look, but at the same time she didn't want to stop looking either. She couldn't not watch. She felt horrified but spellbound at the same time, like a gawker slowing as he drives past some horrendous automobile accident—not wanting to see a mangled body but looking all the same.

Her eyes quickly flew to the patient's face where tears flowed from the corners of her eyes, and Abby could see that she was in terrible pain. The nurse patted the woman's face with a tissue. "Just take a deep breath," the nurse gently coached her. "Breathe, it's almost over," Abby whispered. She wanted to stay focused on the patient, but her eyes shot back to the image on the screen. At first, the baby didn't seem aware of the cannula. It gently prodded the baby's side, and for a quick second Abby felt relief. Of course, she thought, *The fetus doesn't feel pain.* Abby had reassured countless woman of this many times in the past as she had been taught by Planned Parenthood: the fetal tissue feels nothing as it is removed. She began to tell herself, *Get a grip, Abby, this is a simple, quick medical procedure.*

Her thoughts were running wild as she was trying to control her responses but couldn't shake the inner anxiety that was quickly intensifying to horror as she watched the screen. The next movement Abby describes was the sudden jerk of a tiny foot as the baby started kicking, as if trying to move away from the probing intruder. As the cannula pressed in, the baby began struggling to turn and twist away. It seemed clear to Abby that the fetus could feel the instrument and did not like the feeling. And then the doctor's voice broke through, startling her, "Beam me up, Scotty," he said lightheartedly to the nurse. That meant, turn on the suction—in an abortion the suction isn't turned on until the doctor feels he has the cannula in exactly the precise place.

All at once, Abby had a sudden urge to yell, *"Stop!"* And shake the patient, and say, "Look at what is happening to your baby! Wake up! Hurry! Stop them!" But even as Abby thought those words, she looked at her own hand holding the probe and realized she was one of "them" performing this atrocious act. Her eyes immediately shot back to the screen again. The cannula was already being rotated by the doctor and now Abby could see the tiny body violently twisting with it. For the briefest moment, Abby said it looked as if the baby was being wrung like a dishcloth, twirled, and squeezed. And then the little body crumpled and began disappearing into the cannula before her eyes. The last thing Abby saw was the tiny, perfectly formed backbone sucked into the tube and then everything was gone. The uterus was empty. Totally empty.

Abby froze in disbelief and without realizing it, she let go of the probe and it slipped off the patient's tummy onto her leg. Abby felt her heart pounding—pounding so hard her neck throbbed. She tried to take a deep breath but couldn't seem to breathe in or out. She continued to stare at the screen even though it was black now because she had lost the image. Nothing was registering with her. She was too stunned and shaken to move.

She was aware of the doctor and nurse nonchalantly conversing as they worked but it sounded distant, like vague background noise, hard to hear over the pounding of her own blood in her ears. The image of the tiny body, mangled and sucked away, was replaying in her mind along with the image of her daughter's, Grace's, first ultrasound—and how she'd been about the same size. Abby could hear in her memory one of the many arguments she'd had with her husband, Doug, about abortion, "When you were pregnant with Grace, it wasn't a fetus, it was a baby." And now the memory hit her like a lightning bolt, "He was right! What was in that woman's womb just a moment ago was alive! It wasn't just tissue, just cells, that was a human baby—fighting for life! A battle that was lost in the blink of an eye."

What Abby had told people for years, what she'd believed and taught and defended was a lie. Suddenly, she felt the eyes of the doctor and nurse staring at her. It shook her out of her thoughts. She noticed the probe lying on the patient's leg and fumbled to get it back into place. But her hands were shaking now.

"Abby, are you OK?" the doctor asked. The nurse's eyes searched Abby's face with concern. "Yeah, I'm OK." Abby replied. She had not noticed that she didn't have the probe positioned correctly and was worried because the doctor couldn't see inside the uterus. Her right hand held the probe, and her left rested delicately on the patient's warm belly. Abby glanced at the young woman's face and saw there were more tears and a strong expression of pain. Abby moved the probe until she had recaptured the image of the now empty uterus of this young patient. Abby's eyes shot back to her hands. She looked at them as if they weren't even her own.

She had so many heart-wrenching thoughts at that moment: How much damage had her hands participated in over the past eight years? How many lives have been taken because of them? Not just because of her hands, but because of her words. What if she had already known the truth, and what if she'd told all those women? What if? She had believed a lie and blindly promoted the "company line" for so long. Why hadn't she searched out the truth for herself? Why did she close her ears to the arguments she had heard so many times before? Then suddenly, it dawned on her, *Oh, dear God, what have I done?*

With her hand still resting on the young woman's belly, Abby sensed that she had taken something very special from her. She had robbed this young lady of the joy of motherhood. Abby's hand started to hurt, in fact, she began to feel actual physical pain. And right there, standing beside the table with her hand on the weeping young patient's belly, the thought came from deep within her: *Never again! Never again!* And then Abby went into autopilot.

As the nurse cleaned up the young woman, Abby put away the ultrasound machine and then gently awakened the young woman, who was lifeless and dazed. Abby helped her sit up, helped her into a wheelchair and took her to the recovery room. She wrapped a light blanket around her. Like so many patients she had seen before, the young woman continued to cry in apparent emotional and physical pain. Abby did the best she could to make her feel more comfortable. Ten minutes, maybe fifteen at the most, had passed since the nurse practitioner had asked Abby to help in the exam room. And in that short amount of time, everything had changed drastically.

The image of the tiny baby twisting and struggling kept playing over in Abby's mind. Then Abby thought of the patient and she started feeling guilty. A thought ran through Abby's mind, *I have taken something precious from her and she didn't even know it.* Abby asked herself, *How had it come to this and how had I let this happen?*

She had invested herself, her heart, her career in Planned Parenthood because she cared about women in crisis and now, she faced a crisis of her own. Now, after what she had witnessed and experienced, Abby had to come to a place of making a choice: Continue working for an industry of which she had been deceived by all of the lies and deception she had believed for so many years. Or leave and never look back? Anxious and confused, Abby sought help from Shawn Carney, a leader of the local anti-abortion group Coalition for Life with whom she was well-acquainted after his years of activism against Planned Parenthood. She told him she could no longer continue assisting women in getting abortions. She resigned on October 6, 2009. "Empowerment for me as a woman began the day I handed in my resignation to Planned Parenthood."

Today, Abby travels across the globe sharing her story, educating the public on pro-life issues, advocating for the unborn, and reaching out to abortion clinic staff who still work in the industry. She is the founder of And Then There Were None, a ministry designed to assist abortion clinic workers out of the industry. To date, this ministry has helped more than five hundred workers, including seven abortionists, leave the industry. Abby and her husband have eight children.

Chapter 10

A Change of Heart

Dr. Kathi Aultman is a retired OB-GYN and a member of the American College of Obstetricians and Gynecologists. She is currently serving as an Associate Scholar with the Charlotte Lozier Institute.

Kathi grew up a daughter of a Methodist minister and yet she didn't know Jesus until she was thirty-five. Her mom was a typical preacher's wife and was very involved in church and loved making things for church bazaars. Kathi's mom was always taking in anyone who needed help.

As a young girl Kathi loved going to church and enjoyed listening to her dad's sermons. He was a great speaker and told wonderful stories to bring his messages to life. Her dad worked hard, and they didn't see much of him, except for a month in the summer when they all spent time together on a little lake in the woods of North Jersey. Kathi's family lived a transparent life with little to no privacy. She was involved in Sunday school and youth group, but it was more of a social Christianity than an active faith. She knew about God but didn't know God. She saw Jesus only as a good teacher or prophet. The Bible was a mystery to her. She wanted to know more and thought she would find out more when she was confirmed. She had a longing to know God and to have an active vibrant faith, but she wanted proof that God was real. She took confirmation classes, but they were mostly about church history and rules. She remembers hoping that when the bishop laid his hands on her as she knelt at the communion railing somehow everything would miraculously be imparted to her, but she was sadly disappointed. Nothing happened. She slowly came to believe that there was no God and that religion was just an opiate of the people, a way to control them. This was reinforced by the unChristian way people in her congregation treated each other and her father.

Kathi graduated high school and got a scholarship to Drew University where her parents had gone to undergraduate school and her father had gone to seminary. During orientation Kathi's freshman year, a married woman gave her class a talk about sex. Kathi had always believed that one should wait until marriage to have sex, but the female speaker was saying otherwise. She was saying it was OK to have sex prior to marriage. It put a chink in Kathi's armor, and later that year when she became engaged, she had sex for the first time. When the breakup of her engagement occurred, she felt like a fallen woman and ended up having sex with several men that she dated.

When Kathi entered medical school, she believed abortion on demand was a woman's right. This view led to her own decision to have an abortion, a decision she would later deeply regret. She felt that a woman should have control over her own body and not to be forced to bear a child she did not want. She also believed it was wrong to bring unwanted children into an overpopulated world where they might be neglected or abused.

"Medical students and residents are taught that abortion is a normal part of women's health care. The pro-life view is discouraged. It is increasingly difficult for pro-life students to get into medical schools and residency programs, especially OB-GYN. Professors can lose their positions for expressing pro-life views," Kathi explains. She is extremely saddened by the fact that the American College of Obstetricians and Gynecologist, which should be on the front lines fighting for women and the unborn, is actively engaged in opposing pro-life legislation.

Kathi says, "Physicians should be healers not killers."

During her residency program she was trained in first trimester D&C with suction abortions and she obtained special training in second trimester dismemberment abortions. After each procedure Kathi had to examine the tissue to account for all the body parts, to make sure nothing was left to cause infection or bleeding. She was amazed at the perfectly formed organs and limbs with their tiny fingers and toes, and found it fascinating to look at the pathology slides. A human fetus seemed no different to her than the chick embryos she dissected in college. At the time, she could view them from a scientific interest, devoid of any emotions with which she would normally view a baby. She was not heartless; she just had been trained to compartmentalize things. The difference in her mind was whether the baby was wanted or not. If it was wanted, it was a baby, if unwanted it was a fetus. Really! Why should a person's life be dependent on whether someone else wants them or not?

Kathi says, "Pro-abortion groups like Planned Parenthood have brainwashed our society into believing that an unintended pregnancy is the worst thing that can happen to a woman, yet the amount of time needed to keep an unwanted pregnancy after it is discovered, is a very short time to be inconvenienced, when balanced against the entire life of another person."

After Kathi's first year of training, she got a job moonlighting at a clinic doing abortions. She enjoyed the technical challenges of the procedure and prided herself on being good at what she did. She believed she was helping women and did her best to make the procedure as painless as possible for her patients, but she never considered the pain that the baby was experiencing.

The only time she had any qualms about doing abortions was when she realized that she was trying to save babies in the NICU that were the same age as the babies she was aborting. Unfortunately, she was somehow able to rationalize and suppress those feelings.

During her last year of residency, she got pregnant but continued to do abortions without reservations. Her thought at the time was, *My baby is wanted, theirs are not.* The first time she returned to the clinic after she gave birth to her baby, she was confronted with three cases that changed her opinion.

She discovered that she had personally done three abortions on a girl scheduled that morning. When she protested, she was told by the clinic staff that it was her right to choose abortion as her method of birth control, and that Kathi had no right to pass judgement on her, or to refuse to do the procedure. Kathi told them that was fine for them to say, but that she was the one who had to do the killing. The young girl got her abortion, and despite Kathi's urging refused the birth control Kathi offered.

The next situation involved a woman who when asked by her friend if she wanted to see the tissue, replied,

"No! I just want to kill it." Kathi said she felt like saying, "What did that baby do to you?"

The last case literally brought Kathi to tears. This was a mother of four who didn't feel she could support another child. She cried throughout her abortion. That was the end of Kathi's abortion career. She finally made the emotional connection between fetus and baby.

What struck Kathi was the apathy of the first patient and the hostility of the second toward her baby, contrasted with the sorrow and misery of the woman who knew what it was like to have a child.

Kathi eventually realized that the baby was the innocent victim in all of this. The fact that the baby was unwanted was no longer enough justification for her to kill it.

Kathi says, "Few doctors can do abortions for very long. Although women seeking abortions are told that the pregnancy is just a blob of tissue, the abortionist knows exactly what he or she is doing because they must count the body parts. Eventually the truth sinks in. It is especially difficult for ob/gyns because they are normally concerned about the welfare of both their patients, but in an abortion, they are killing one of them."

Sadly, although Kathi could not personally do abortions anymore, she remained a staunch supporter of abortion rights. She maintained her beliefs even after becoming a Christian. Her views began to change because she saw women who did extremely well after deciding to keep their baby and those who struggled with the emotional and physical complications of abortion. That wasn't what she was expecting. It was inconsistent with the feminist rhetoric she had embraced.

The other thing that began to chip away at her pro-abortion armor was watching precious children in her church, who were almost aborted, grow up. Interacting with them made her realize that those unwanted preborn babies each had their own unique personality.

She did not completely change her opinion on abortion. She continued to advocate for it and encouraged women that it was their choice.

Thankfully, Christian friends accepted her despite her views on abortion. Her heart was changed when one of them was brave enough to give her an article comparing abortion to the Holocaust. The article shook Kathi because her father had accompanied the unit that liberated the first concentration camp during WWII, and she grew up with those stories and pictures. She could never understand how the Nazis could do what they did, but as she reflected on her previous actions and beliefs, she understood how they were able to coolly exterminate so many people and how physicians justified the atrocious experiments they performed in the name of science. Just as she did not consider fetuses as humans, they did not consider Jews and others as human beings. She realized that she was no better than the people she abhorred; she was a mass murderer. That was when she finally changed her opinion on abortion and became pro-life.

Healing took a lot of prayer and counseling. She went to the Christian Healing Center in Jacksonville, Florida, where a counselor, who was also a member of her church, prayed with her. Kathi understood that God forgave her, but she struggled to forgive herself. It took God asking her this question, "Kathi, are you more powerful than I am that I can forgive you, but you cannot forgive yourself?" Tears poured down her face as she was overwhelmed by the grace of God.

Another holocaust, abortion, is going on today throughout the world under the guise of helping women. Kathi is now helping not only the women in circumstances of unplanned pregnancies, but also saving the lives of the precious innocent babies inside the womb of those women.

Are we going to close our ears to the cries of these innocent babies, just as they did in World War II as the Jews were being carted off to incinerators? Will we as Christians just sit in our pews in church and sing our worship songs louder and louder to drown out the cries of babies on their way to abortion mills throughout the world and just say, "It's a woman's choice," or will we rise up and tell the truth of abortion as Kathi is doing?

Below is a very touching poem the Lord gave Kathi just after she agreed to speak at the March for Life in Washington, DC.

Hello Mommy, I'm Here! It's Me!

I am so glad to be here! What a wonderful place! Your heartbeat soothes me as I float, cozy and warm. The rhythm of your movement rocks me to sleep. I love you, Mommy!

You don't know I'm here yet, and I can't wait for you to find out. I know you will be excited to get as wonderful a gift as me. God picked me especially for you.

I long to meet you. I've been tapping on your tummy hoping you will notice me. I'm here, Mommy. It's me!

It's getting a bit squishy in here now, but it gives me a chance to feel my body against yours and feel your touch. Sometimes I can hear your lovely voice. I love it when you laugh and sing. Mmmm, was that chocolate you just ate? How nice it is to be here. How nice it is to be me!

Why are you crying, Mommy? I thought you would be happy to know I was here. I might be inconvenient, but it will all work out. Wait and see. God has a plan. Does it really matter how I came to be? I'm here, Mommy! It's me!

I only need to stay a little while 'til I can be on my own. Won't you give me a chance? I can be a blessing if you let me. I'm yours, Mommy! It's me!

If you really can't keep me, let me bless

*someone else. Listen to your heart. Don't
kill me, Mommy! I'm here! It's me!*

*Give me a chance to see who I can be. There
is no guarantee that I'll be perfect, but I will
be unique. I'm here, Mommy! It's me!*

*Perhaps I will be an artist or a geologist.
Maybe I will find a cure for cancer or
broker of peace that keeps us from war.
You will never know if you kill me!*

*Don't listen to those who say I'm just a blob
of tissue. I'm real, Mommy! I'm me!
I have hopes and dreams and a will
to live. Give me the chance to see a
rainbow and hear the birds sing, to
taste lemonade and smell a rose.*

*I want to run and jump and tumble in the
grass. I want to feel the warmth of the sun
on my face. I'm here, Mommy! It's me!*

*Let me stay just a little longer. When I
am strong enough, I will leave. I know
there are others who can love me if you
cannot keep me, and I will thank you
for your mercy and sacrifice. Please let
me live, Mommy! Let me be me!*

I'm here, Mommy! It's me!

Chapter 11

Born Out of the Heart of God

Bob and Audrey had an ideal marriage. In fact, their marriage was the kind that most people dreamed of having. Bob and Audrey unquestionably loved doing life together. Bob said, "We would talk about everything, all the time, just sharing our lives, our hopes and dreams together. I was completely captivated by her." Audrey felt safe with Bob because he loves God, and she felt she could be with him forever. The two were pastoring a church and working for Audrey's mom and dad in their TV ministry. Bob said, "I had no idea how hard it would be."

Like most newly married couples, a few months into marriage Audrey realized that Bob's communication style was completely different than hers. Audrey said, "He could easily confront me if something was wrong." So, she made a vow that she would do everything possible so that he would never yell at her again. Therefore, Audrey became the ultimate performer and the ultimate pleaser.

At the time, they were hosting their own television program and the busy demands and hard work of ministry was very exhausting and began to take a toll on Audrey. She began stuffing her feelings deep down inside of her because she knew Bob loved the church and she could never tell him how she truly felt.

Seventeen years into their marriage, a young man started coming to church. He became friendly with Bob and Audrey's family. He spent more and more time at their house. He was energetic and lively and liked being with their children. Bob said, "This young man didn't have a family, so it was very natural at the beginning to invite him to join our family for the holidays."

This young man began paying more attention to Audrey, flirting with her. She thought, *We need to find you a girlfriend.* Audrey said, "He was fun, he was young, and he reminded me of being a kid again."

Audrey was thirty-six with three kids, ten, twelve, and fifteen years old, but the way he looked at her, and the things he said to her, such as, "You're so beautiful. I want to find someone in this world that could even be half as amazing as you" caused something within Audrey's heart to gravitate toward him. She thought, *That's what I need.* Audrey knew there was no way she would do anything inappropriate, never mind having an affair. Audrey thought, *I can go in the same car with him. I don't have to have boundaries that other people have because I'm in control.* She had convinced herself his friendship could never be a problem. Spiritual pride shows up when we don't think we need God in certain situations. Audrey made the choice to give in and became friends with this guy. They started having fun together. What she didn't realize was that sin would take her further than she ever dreamed it could go.

Audrey said, "Our shoulders would bump, or his hand would touch mine, and I started noticing my reaction to that." She thought, *Oh that felt good when he touched me.* She told herself, *I can have it all. This relationship won't really affect the rest of my life.* She found herself lying to herself so that she could be alone with him. Audrey just plunged in headfirst and said, "You know what, I've gone this far anyway so I'm just going to do this." And that's when it became sexual. Audrey said, "I just lied to the people I love most so I could get away with this guy and be inappropriate sexually and have this secret affair. This is not me." The sexual affair lasted three weeks. Audrey realized that she couldn't stomach the double life she was living and finally ended the affair.

Now she had to face her husband of seventeen years and tell him what she had done. She was petrified out of her mind thinking about how Bob would react. She was shaking. Audrey said, "If it came down to a 'choice' of who she would choose, there was never a question in her mind." She wanted her husband and her kids. Audrey had not even confronted Bob on the little things in their marriage and now here she was, about to tell him the most betraying message you could ever imagine. Audrey finally mustered up enough nerve to tell him. She sat very close to him and whispered in Bob's ear and said, "I've done something unpleasantly inappropriate." The look on Bob's face was extreme anger and hatred.

Bob found himself wanting to punch holes in walls, slam doors, somehow express the anger and rage he was feeling inside. He said, "This wasn't just some tiny little mistake or setback in our marriage." As Audrey knelt before him crying and confessing her sin of adultery, Bob began to wonder, *What am I to do? Here I am a spiritual leader in our community, a pastor.* In Bob's mind, he had no answers. Immediately, he began to create a rescue plan for his life and instantly thought, *I'm leaving.* At that time, Bob wanted Audrey to be exposed for what she had done to him and their family. Suddenly, he took on the role of victim. Bob said, "I'm the innocent one here, so I wanted to gather everyone around me to be able to show what she did to me." Bob left the room, not knowing what to do. He called a pastor friend, and he said, "Bob, let's talk later this evening." He then asked Bob, "Who knows?" Bob told him, "Nobody." His friend said, "Good, let's keep it that way."

That wasn't what Bob was thinking. He wanted everybody involved because he was the innocent one here. Bob said, "This wasn't something that we'll just get over or through this and everything will quickly be OK."

That evening his friend began to speak to him about the principle of covenant. Bob's thoughts the whole time were, *I just want to expose her.* The pastor friend said, "But the Father's heart is to cover. Covering has two primary principles; Proverbs 25:2 *'It's God's glory to conceal a matter and for a king to discover its understanding.'* To cover is to protect, and secondly, to promote healing. You see, when we come to God, He doesn't shame us, He doesn't expose us, rather He gathers us in, and He loves us and He covers us. He doesn't leave us there. He says, 'I want to heal you. You see, I don't want your past to determine your future.' He says, 'I want my love and grace to determine your future.'" So, he began to speak to Bob of the Father's heart, and he asked, "Will you have that for your wife?"

Bob wanted to escape, he wanted to just get out. Bob said, "I wanted to sleep on the couch that very first night I found out, even go get a hotel room. All I knew was that I wanted to leave." But the counsel that came from the pastor was this: "No, you're going to get right back into your marriage bed tonight, and you will not spend one night apart from each other, because we will not participate with the spirit of divorce; that's hard, but you see, that is my Father's heart." Bob was faced with a choice. Does he let the awful choice his wife made to have an affair tear apart his home and family? Or does he follow the advice his pastor friend was giving him? Even though the easy choice would have been for Bob to remain angry and point fingers at Audrey and tell her, "You're the one with the problem!" Bob knew he had to do whatever he had to for his marriage and family to stay together. The pastor also told him that he and Audrey should pray together.

Bob said, "The only words we could get out were, 'God, we need You.' And we just cried and cried." Audrey said, "Every part of our relationship had to come to a new level of transparency. There was no room for any secrets."

Bob and Audrey resigned from their positions of pastoring with the television ministry and went into a place of safety to get help for their family. God supernaturally provided for them with work and a home. Bob said, "I didn't know if we would ever be happy again a day in our lives, but I knew that divorce was not the answer."

One More Secret Revealed

A couple months later, Bob and Audrey received mind-blowing news from the doctor. Audrey was pregnant. They both were at a loss for words. Bob had had a vasectomy, so he knew it wasn't his. The doctor must have seen the look of fear on both of their faces because he immediately asked, "Do you want to continue with this pregnancy?"

Bob had so many questions: "Would I be able to love this baby as my own? I know what it's like to have a small child crawl up your leg, and look into your eyes and say, 'Daddy' and I knew what my heart was, and it was not to be your daddy." Bob knew the transformation it would take. The natural love he and Audrey once had, had faded, and it wasn't sufficient to take them where they needed to be. They needed God's supernatural love. But Bob immediately answered the doctor, "Yes, without a doubt."

Bob said, "Before, everything inside of me wanted to punish Audrey. Now, I recognized that she's carrying a baby and that she needed my help. This baby's going to need parents. I want to be that dad." God can take a heart of hurt and anger and give you a heart of flesh so that you can understand His heart for what you are going through, just as He did for Bob. Ezekiel 36:26 says, *"I will give you a new heart and put a new spirit in you; I will remove from you your heart of stone and give you a heart of flesh"* (NIV).

Audrey, however, was in a desperate situation, and she never thought she could even contemplate abortion. She was a Jesus girl and had been in ministry. She had so many thoughts, *Now my kids are going to be messed up. I'm going to be disqualified. I'm going to be known for the most stupid and selfish choice I've ever made.* Audrey remembers exactly where she was in her kitchen when she made the phone call to the abortion clinic. She dialed the number. When a young lady came on the line, Audrey began telling her the circumstances. The young lady said, "No problem. We can send you ten pills in the mail and just take one pill every week and the problem will be over." Audrey hung up the phone, and thought, *I don't know if that is the answer, but I know I can't live through this. I can't live through the whole idea. I'm so scared.* Audrey fell on her knees and said, "God, I won't have an abortion, but I'm begging You, if You love me, You will give me a miscarriage, because I can't carry this." Audrey is thankful that God didn't answer that prayer. "What I was truly praying for was God to eject me out of my circumstances." But God in His love said, "Audrey, I'm going to walk with you through every moment."

A Baby Brother

Bob and Audrey called a meeting with their three children to let them know what was going on. Bob and Audrey were in their bedroom when the door opened, and the children saw their mom and dad sitting on the floor crying. Bob immediately got up and pulled a large queen-size blanket from the bed. With Audrey seated on the floor, he took the blanket and covered her from head to foot and then knelt beside her and wrapped his arms around her. Bob looked deep into his children's eyes and said, "Kids, this is what God does when we make a mistake. He comes to us, He covers us, and He wraps His arms around us, and He says, 'I will never leave you; I will never forsake you.'" With Audrey covered in Bob's arms, he looked in their eyes and said, "I love your mom. She's so precious to us. I am not going anywhere. We are a family. We belong with each other. Kids, you're going to have a baby brother." Suddenly, the older two children began to cry, but their thirteen-year-old daughter just smiled as big as anything. She looked up at Bob and said, "Daddy, we're having a baby!" That was when Bob knew that they were all going to be OK.

Several months later, it was time for this little baby boy to be born. What did they name the baby? Bob said, "I gave him my name, Robert. His middle name is Theodore, which means 'divine gift.'" Bob was once asked if Robert was a gift. Bob answered, "He's not an accident. He's not a mistake. He's not a result of a sexual affair. He was born out of the heart of God, just as my other three children, and entrusted to me. He is the greatest gift, and one of the greatest gifts I've ever received."

Audrey said, "Oh, he's just brought so much joy to our home, and I think back...to all the lies the enemy told me about my kids being messed up and that we would never laugh again or dream again." There were times it felt as though the enemy had sucked the breath out of their family, but God, in His mercy and grace, breathed new breath into this family and gave them hope to live life to its fullest.

Chapter 12

SILENT NO MORE

SOME BELIEVE ONLY WOMEN HAVE THE RIGHT to choose whether to carry a baby to term. It's true that women have the option to choose right or wrong, but this right doesn't exempt them from the consequences. They are not the only ones to suffer. Let's not forget the father of the baby. It doesn't matter if he encouraged the abortion or not; he too will suffer the consequences. Grandparents' hearts are broken because they weren't given the chance to know their grandchild. Siblings are hurt because they lost a sibling. Friends who may have tried to ease the pain by assuring the woman it's OK to abort will feel the effects. The shock waves of abortion diminish the family in our society as women choose careers over children. It causes trauma that sometimes leads to substance abuse, suicidal actions, and risk-taking behavior affecting not just the parents of the child, but also the community around them. Since this decision affects so many, how can it just be a personal and private choice between only a woman and her doctor?

Irene met her husband in the eighth grade. Two years later they were sweethearts and got married. At sixteen Irene gave birth to their first daughter and soon had five more daughters. The next several years proved to be a struggle for them financially, physically, and emotionally.

She was working part time while attending school full time, and her husband was working full time, but they still had trouble making ends meet and taking care of their six daughters. Looking back, Irene realized that one of the reasons they had such a hard time was they stopped going to church. She says, "That was the biggest mistake of our lives, and the beginning of the destruction of our family."

Life was hectic and demanding. With work and school, Irene was away from the home a lot. This put an extreme burden on her husband. She says, "We were way too busy, even to the point that we had no time for the Lord in our lives." Romantic evenings of laughing, cuddling, and having fun together turned into arguing over the simplest little things. The arguments led to blaming and resenting each other, so Irene and her husband separated. Their children were left with no father in the home.

During the separation from her husband, Irene was desperate and confused. Her life was in despair, and she had an affair with a childhood friend. Soon she discovered she was pregnant with that man's baby.

Irene knew in her heart that she still loved her husband wanted to reconcile with him. They got back together when she was about four months pregnant. They planned to raise the baby themselves, but the biological father did not agree with this plan and refused to sign the adoption papers.

During the pregnancy, Irene rubbed her stomach and talked to her baby. She told her, "Mama's going to make it all better! I love you, my darling little one." However, Irene was so desperate to have her family back together, to see her six daughters happy again. Irene thought that if she had an abortion, everything would be fine. At the time she thought, "No one will know about this." Irene says, "Boy, was I ever wrong!"

Irene went to a Planned Parenthood Clinic, but at just over twenty-five weeks, she was too far along for them to do the abortion. They referred her to an affiliate in Los Angeles. Frightened and unsure of herself, Irene just wanted someone to tell her it was going to be OK. She came from a large family, but she had never felt more alone in her life.

Irene began telling God how sorry she was. She had been raised Catholic and knew what she was doing, but at the time she was so distraught. She began telling her daughter she was carrying, "It's OK! You're going to heaven, and you know you're going to be with God. I'm getting you out of this world, because nobody loves you here." But that was a lie! Irene did everything in her mind to justify why she had to walk into that clinic. She was still torn as she was on the way there; she told herself that if there were sidewalk counselors there, she wouldn't go through with it. But when she drove up, there weren't any sidewalk counselors there that day.

At that moment, Irene felt as if she were a zombie. As she walked into the clinic, she was crying and upset, but no one ask if she was OK. Once she got inside the building, she immediately felt like part of a herd, as if she had a number on her back and a dollar sign on her face. She began to sob and was unable to engage in simple conversation. The staff gave her a gown to put on and told her to wait in the room where the other women were. A nurse took her vitals. Irene noticed that a television was on in the room. She couldn't comprehend what she was seeing; it puzzled her that these women were watching it and laughing and joking as if everyone was in denial about what was about to happen to them. Weeping, Irene sat rubbing her stomach, saying, "I'm sorry, I'm so sorry!" They called her back into another room, laid her on a narrow gurney. The room was cold and dreary.

The young lady assisting the abortionist saw Irene's face and said to the abortionist, "Wow! Look at her eyes, how frightened she is." The abortionist asked Irene if this was her first abortion. Irene answered with a shaky voice "Yes, it is." The abortionist responded, "Oh, don't worry, it's not a big deal." Irene learned later that this was the biggest lie she had ever heard. *It's not a big deal? Yeah, right!* runs through Irene's mind daily.

As the doctor administered the chemical drug into her belly, Irene was mortified and shocked when she felt her baby kick, twist, and turn, fighting for her life. Everything became clear to Irene, *Oh my God! What am I doing? There is life; that's my child, my baby inside of me.* They took Irene laid her on a table in another room with the other women. They weren't laughing or talking now. Everyone was silent and crying. Irene could see the tears flowing down their faces.

Thirty minutes later, after giving Irene something sweet to eat and orange juice to drink, they told her to come back the next day. Since Irene was so far along in her pregnancy, aborting was a multiday process. Irene was too traumatized by the experience. She wouldn't be coming back.

When Irene left the clinic, she immediately went to the labor and delivery department at the local hospital, hoping to save her daughter's life. The medical staff hooked her up to a monitor, and initially the doctor told her that her baby was going to be OK since they detected a healthy heartbeat. Unfortunately, a couple hours later, they told her that the chemical they had been injected would deteriorate the baby's heart; the damage was irreversible, and there was nothing they could do. They encouraged her to return to the clinic.

Irene refused. It had been too traumatizing. She returned to the hospital the next day, and they induced labor. After seven hours, Irene gave birth to a beautiful, yet lifeless girl, Leonor Bridgette Beltran. The nurse placed her on Irene's chest; Irene stroked her tiny little face. "She looked exactly like a newborn baby; except she was smaller." She fit in the palm of Irene's hand. Irene says, "Everything was intact." Crying, Irene asked her daughter for forgiveness, "I'm so sorry. Mom was scared. Mom didn't know what else to do. I am so sorry. I love you."

Irene, her parents, and other family members were able to hold the baby and spend time with her. After a couple hours, a nurse came into the room; it was time for her to take the baby. Irene wrapped and swaddled Leonor. She hugged her sweet, precious daughter one last time and said, "Goodbye. I love you until I see you again," and then gave her to the nurse. Now Irene, her family, and the biological father's family were left with the daunting task of planning Leonor's funeral. They buried Leonor Bridgette Beltran at the local cemetery where Irene and her family now visit her.

After this experience, Irene made a commitment to the Lord to devote her life to the sanctity of life, to help minimize or eliminate the victims of abortion. She has such a heart of compassion to help women not feel damaged, humiliated, or hopelessness after an abortion. Irene says, "Women truly deserve better than abortion." She knows that the Lord, Leonor, and her family have forgiven her, and she has forgiven herself. And she wants other women to feel and know that same forgiveness.

Irene's choice left countless people grief-stricken. She put not only her daughter through a painful death, but she also robbed her other children of a sister that they could have played with, fed, and helped nurture. Three sets of grandparents will never watch a granddaughter grow up. Future generations will not exist because Irene made the choice to destroy the life of her daughter, and her future children, their children, and so on. "I am compelled to tell Leonor's story to protect America's children and their mothers, fathers, and siblings."

Irene is now the regional coordinator for Silent No More Awareness in Los Angeles, California. She and her family are active in the pro-life movement. At local abortion clinics and various pro-life events they hold up signs that say, "I Regret My Abortion," "I Mourn My Aborted Sibling," and "I Regret Losing My Grandchild to Abortion." It's important to them that people know the ugly truth. Irene says, "Abortion is not a quick fix, but instead, a lifetime of consequences." They are a voice for Leonor and the countless innocent babies who cannot speak for themselves.

Chapter 13

THE BLUE-EYED LITTLE BOY

MONICA WAS AN ACTIVE YOUNG GIRL WHO grew up moving a lot due to her father's military career. She battled insecurity; she never felt good enough or pretty enough. Living in a constant state of comparison, she longed to know that she was enough for somebody, to feel truly accepted. As many girls do, she looked for this acceptance in relationships.

Monica thought she had found what she was looking for when she started dating. Understand that her parents were attentive and loved her, but she still looked for love from others. When she met a young man who was older than her and who showed her attention, she was willing to do whatever she had to in order to keep his attention. The young man was a good kid and treated her very well. Her mother objected to her dating for obvious reasons. Her parents believed she was too young to date and also felt that there was too much of an age difference between the two. Needless to say, this probably drove her even more to date him. She definitely had a bit of rebellion in her and told her mother that she was going to date him despite what she said.

The two became promiscuous, and she got pregnant. Not knowing what to do, her parents sought to seek advice by taking her to a women's clinic. While there a nurse told them that she was too young to have a baby and that she would probably die if she tried because her body wasn't ready for that. The nurse also told them that it was just a blob of tissue and that it wasn't a formed baby yet. Naturally, Monica's instinct and mind immediately thought, *I don't want to die.* So they told the boyfriend that they were going to proceed with the abortion. He agreed and offered to pay since he felt it was his responsibility to do so.

The appointment was scheduled, and the day arrived. As Monica walked into the clinic, she was handed paperwork to fill out and a pill to take. She was then called back for the procedure. She had no idea what was about to occur and the impact it would have on her life. Upon changing into a paper gown, the nurse helped her up on the table and told her to lay back and relax. The nurse held her hand during the procedure and told her everything would be OK and that it would all be over soon and everything would be all better. The next thing Monica remembers is sitting in a chair, cramping badly. She went home and slept for what felt like for days. It was never discussed. Life just went on.

Two years later, at sixteen, she got pregnant again. Thoughts ran through her head wondering how she ended up in this situation again. What was she going to do this time? What were her parents going to do? Were they going to kill her or disown her? She knew that they would be so angry and highly disappointed. Overcome with shame and tremendous fear, she could barely even think. Her world felt like it was completely closing in. She did not want to have to face her parents again. She desperately wanted to run away and not have to deal with this again. After revealing to her parents that she was pregnant, they were extremely disappointed. The pressure of fighting with her boyfriend's parents about the pregnancy pushed her to make the decision to abort once again. After already having had one abortion having another one didn't seem so bad. If she had an abortion, nobody would have to worry about anything.

She made an appointment, but this time it did not go as planned. Once inside the procedure room something very unusual happened. The abortionist told her that he could not do the procedure because she was too far along. Never have I ever heard of a doctor who said they would not do an abortion procedure. You need to understand. This is their job, how they make money. When the doctor told her that he couldn't do the procedure, she was shocked. She even argued a little saying that she wasn't too far along. But he refused, and she left the abortion clinic. She kept wondering what she was supposed to do, but she knew in her heart that she was going to keep the baby and raise it.

So time came for her to give birth and off to the hospital she went. She was scheduled for an induction for fear that the baby maybe too big. Her parents were there and her boyfriend at the time. Her labor was hard and she had no pain meds. The baby was stuck because she was a bit big and her arm was in the way. After several hours she finally delivered a beautiful, seven-pound eleven-ounce baby girl. She became the most loved little girl ever, and Monica's world was forever changed. Little did she know that was just the beginning of a new life!

The day she delivered, a lady came to her hospital room and brought a gift to her. She had never met the woman; a school friend of Monica's had told the woman about her being pregnant. God had laid Monica on her heart, and she wanted to come meet her. While visiting, she invited Monica to a Bible study. She agreed to come in a couple of weeks. When Monica got to the Bible study, she found that the group of ladies had thrown a beautiful baby shower. She was shocked and taken aback because all she ever felt were people judging her. She couldn't believe that a group of strangers would throw her a baby shower. She felt so loved and accepted. She never once felt judged or condemned. They talked to her about accepting Jesus as her Lord and Savior and she did. She remembers thinking that she had never met a God who was so loving; the only God she ever knew was angry and distant. But because of the love these women had shown her, she was able to see God for who He really is. She immediately fell in love with Jesus and to this day is still so in love with Him.

She continued going to Bible study. One night a girl she had never seen before came. That night the girl confessed that she had had an abortion. As the group was getting ready to pray for her, the leaders asked if anyone else had ever had an abortion and had not asked for forgiveness. Monica's heart began to pound; all she could think was, "How am I to tell these women that I had an abortion?" She just knew that they would judge her. As she slowly raised her hand, she looked around the room waiting for the look of disappointment, but instead she saw their eyes full of compassion. As she and the other girl prayed for God to forgive them, Monica saw the face of a little boy. She thought maybe she was just imagining things. But when she got home and began to share with her mother about asking God for forgiveness and the image that she saw, her mother said she had seen the same image. When she asked her mother how she knew, her mother explained that when she had asked God for forgiveness for her part in Monica's abortion, God had shown her the same little boy. They knew that God showed them the same image as a sign of confirmation.

Monica eventually married the father of her daughter, and they had a son. But after about ten years, they divorced. Several years later, she remarried. She had two more children, and then they moved to Georgia. She was working at a church and volunteering at a Pregnancy Care Center. To fulfill their training requirements for working at the center, the director, another volunteer, and Monica drove up to Augusta, Georgia.

Before the trip Monica had been battling some physical issues along with anxiety and panic attacks. She would wake up in a sweat with her heart racing in the middle of the night feeling terrified that she wouldn't see the light of day. She always felt like she was having a heart attack. She had gone to the doctor numerous times, but they could never find anything wrong with her. Monica realized she was under spiritual attack, and had learned to overcome. So when they were in Augusta, she was surprised when a wave of sadness would come over her when they were in a particular part of town. It wasn't until the last day of their trip that she remembered that that area was where she had gone to have the abortion.

After the trip, one day in prayer she felt that the Lord impressed on her to go to the abortion clinic. She knew she had already been forgiven. She didn't need closure, and she didn't need to set up a memorial. So she couldn't understand why God was asking her to go. But she wanted to be obedient. After explaining to her husband what she felt, they agreed that since they going to be in area for a friend's wedding, they would stop. The wedding was on Saturday, November 2, 2013. On Sunday, November 3, 2013, as they started to make their way toward the clinic, her heart began to race so fast; all she could do was just pray. Her husband parked the car and told her that he and the children would stay in the car.

There was no one around. As soon as she stepped onto the grass in front of the clinic, she immediately saw the enemy standing to her left. He began to hurl accusations at her, saying that she needed to die and that she needed to pay the price for what she had done. She had taken a life and she needed to pay with her life. As she stood there, she saw and felt the Lord Jesus standing on her right side. He gently yet firmly spoke to her and told her that He had already paid the price for what she had done and that He died in her place. He revealed to her that a curse of death had been spoken over her when she went for the abortion. Remember, the nurse told her she could die if she tried to have the baby. Our words have power, and we need to be careful how we use them.

The Lord then told her to tell the enemy all that the Lord had said and to break the curse of death that was spoken over her. As she did, the enemy disappeared, and she felt the peace of God. God then showed her what happened to her in the spirit on the day of the abortion.

As she wept and asked God to heal her, He brought complete wholeness. When she finally felt that God was done, she opened her eyes, and in the flesh was a blonde hair, blue-eyed little boy standing in front of her smiling from ear to ear. She was taken aback because she didn't know where he had come from. His parents were just a few feet ahead of him and kept calling him to come to them. But he just stood there and smiled at her. After a few moments, his father called him again and he ran off and grabbed his father's hand. They began to walk away, and he looked back and smiled one more time.

When Monica got back in the car, her husband asked if she had seen the little boy. He was just like the little boy that God had shown her when she had asked for forgiveness at the Bible study. She never understood the doors she opened spiritually when she had the abortion. She knew that she had been forgiven, and she knew God was healing her. But until that day she had no idea that God was going to heal her completely and make her whole. And because God is a God of details and leaves nothing undone, all this happened on the day of her daughter's birthday, twenty-five years after her abortion. You can't tell Monica that God isn't awesome!

To this day Monica lives completely surrendered to God. She desires to please Him and bring healing and wholeness to others who have been wounded by the enemy. She and her husband have a wonderful marriage that glorifies God. All her children love the Lord, and she has been blessed with six beautiful grandchildren who are growing up to love the Lord.

Chapter 14

A PRECIOUS GIFT

AT TWENTY-SIX YEARS OLD, VICTORIA FOUND herself in a traumatic place in her life. She was married to an abusive man. They were married for about a year and nine months when they separated. There was a lot of struggles right from the beginning of the marriage. Victoria's husband at the time was an addict and had a violent nature.

Victoria's heart was to work on the marriage, but she knew she could not do it by herself, so she gave her husband an ultimatum. She knew the only way the marriage would work would be if they went to counseling, either together or separately. Victoria says, "I knew the marriage wouldn't work if we both were not willing to work on our issues."

After giving her husband the ultimatum, Victoria came home one day to find that he had packed all his things and he just left.

While they were still together, Victoria decided to get help because she was struggling emotionally. She ended up going to a therapist, which was very unusual for her because she had stuffed so much inside over the years of her own life. Because of all the hurts and disappointments that she had gone through herself, it wasn't easy for Victoria to open up to anyone, but she decided to go to a therapist anyway. During this time, she didn't know the Lord.

She began seeing the therapist and started sharing things with him about her life, such as things that had happened with her dad and how she was raised. She also shared about her current situation. Victoria says, "I can't say I found any true healing or release; I think it just felt good to talk about it for the first time, just to share something." Victoria began opening her heart up to this man, her therapist, and really trusting him with some extremely deep things.

However, a short while later, her therapist was to leave the company he was with. He told Victoria he couldn't see her anymore, but that she could see another therapist.

Because of company policy, the therapist couldn't tell Victoria where he was going. So Victoria said "OK" but she knew that she couldn't bear to share her heart with another therapist. It had been extremely difficult for her to open up to one person and she thought, *That pretty much isn't going to happen.* She just wasn't going to do that.

A short time later, because he had all of Victoria's information, he ended up contacting her and wanted to come to her house and he did. He started pursuing Victoria and they started having relations together. At the time Victoria's husband wasn't with her, but she was still legally married to him.

She was having relations with her therapist, however learned that there was a lot of deception going on. Victoria found out that he was a married man. He told Victoria that he wasn't with his wife anymore, but she found out later that was a lie as well. Victoria was in this relationship with this man, but noticed that he wasn't around much, only when it was convenient for him.

Early in the relationship Victoria found out she was pregnant. She was 28. She remembers her mom saying, "Aren't you a little old to be getting into trouble?" And she thought to herself, *Yea, I guess I am.*

Here she was, pregnant by her ex-therapist and he didn't want her to have the baby. He wanted her to abort the child. He was adamant about it, so he began threatening her during the time of her pregnancy. He persistently pressured her to abort the child. Victoria said she knew he was fearful, because he was a therapist and because he had stepped over the line in pursuing a relationship with Victoria, aborting the baby was a way of protecting himself. He ended up using the things that Victoria had confided in him confidentially. He threatened to use them against her to make her look like an unfit mother and take her baby.

During this time there were a lot of threats and Victoria was fearful for her and her baby's life, because his true nature began to show.

About eight weeks into the pregnancy Victoria found out her brother had committed suicide. During that time Victoria never talked about her pregnancy with anyone. She didn't want people knowing she was pregnant. She walked in such shame from being pregnant and wanting to hide it. She never looked information up about pregnancy or anything about the stages that you would go through. Victoria found herself in such distress that she didn't even want to know. She was in a horrible state of mind.

In the meantime, her husband that she was still married to, started coming back around wanting to talk to her. He became very violent. One night he came over to her house and she was terrified because he was outside her door. At the time Victoria lived in a trailer and the doors weren't that strong. He pounded on her door so hard that the door on the inside started splintering and falling apart. He was screaming and yelling, "Let me in!" Victoria didn't because she was afraid. He was upset because he had just found out that Victoria was pregnant, and he began threatening her.

Not only was Victoria's husband at the time angry about the pregnancy, her one brother, who was prejudiced, was also angry that she was pregnant by a man whose skin color was a little darker than theirs. She was surrounded by angry people and she felt very unsafe.

During this time one of Victoria's good friends who she really trusted and valued her opinion said to her, "Maybe you shouldn't have this child, maybe you should have an abortion because this could ruin your life." There was so much chaos going on in Victoria's life that not only did she contemplate what her friend was saying to her, she scheduled an appointment to have the abortion.

Victoria's mom had been through so much herself. Her daughter, Victoria's sister, died in a horrible house fire tragically at the young age of 12. She had gotten trapped in the fire in the house they all grew up in and couldn't get out.

Fifteen years later, Victoria's brother Tony at thirty years old committed suicide, causing her mom to go completely numb, to the point of psychologically checking out. Therefore, Victoria felt all alone, not just emotionally but also financially. She was barely getting by and wasn't sure how she was going to make everything work. Victoria was in a great deal of despair, so devastated by the death of her brother that she was eaten up with guilt because she was already eight weeks pregnant and she had never told her brother. She started thinking, *Well perhaps if I would have told him, maybe he wouldn't have done it, if he knew I was having a baby*

After that happened, she just didn't care who knew anymore, but deep down inside she did care. This was Victoria's way of functioning in life. Just not caring anymore, her brother was gone, and she still felt scared and alone. She still didn't go around bragging about it. (Telling people she was pregnant.)

As time went on, Victoria made the decision not to have the abortion but to have the baby. You may ask the question, "What stopped Victoria from having the abortion?" Victoria reveals yet another deep dark secret that in the end God brought healing to her life and gave her a second chance. You see our God is a God of second chances, even third and fourth chances because of His amazing transforming love. Even if you think you've gone too far, His love can reach you just as He did with Victoria.

Looking back, at the age of fifteen, Victoria's parents had divorced, but Victoria says she is not sure which happened first—her sister being trapped and dying in the fire or if she got pregnant first. She says, "All I know was it all happened at once." The atmosphere was extremely violent throughout Victoria's childhood. Victoria's mom, Victoria, and her siblings were continuously beaten, and their lives threatened. They suffered so much abuse no child should ever have to endure. Victoria's upbringing wasn't easy.

Victoria's mom finally got up enough courage and money to leave her father. At the time of the house fire Victoria's father was in a mental ward at the VA Hospital because he wasn't well. While he was in the hospital, Victoria's brother and sister were at the childhood home that they no longer lived at, but it was still there. Victoria's father wasn't home at the time, so her brother and sister went there, and that night was when the house burned. Victoria's brother got out, but her sister did not.

There was a boy that started pursuing Victoria and at 15, the one time they had sex together, Victoria got pregnant. Victoria found herself scared and distraught. She decided to tell her mom she was pregnant. Victoria's mom had a lot of things going on in her head at the time. She thought, *Well, I'm calling my cousin, he lives in Florida.* She had planned on sending Victoria to Florida to hide it, so she could have the baby then give the baby away. Victoria is not sure what happened, but her mother decided that she would pay for Victoria to have an abortion. Victoria's mother scheduled the appointment at the clinic. Victoria went in and had the abortion. Victoria says she remembers the next day going back to school knowing what she had done. Victoria felt horrible about what she had done. Victoria went through her whole life not telling anyone.

After divorcing her first husband and being pursued by another man, she ended up marrying another man;

they were together a total of sixteen years but married for twelve. That was the only father that Victoria's daughter Brittani knew.

After marrying this man, Victoria felt comfortable to tell him about her abortion she had when she was fifteen years old. At that time, it was the very first time, all those years later that she confessed it to someone, because of the shame. Even then Victoria was full of shame; she still wasn't free. But it was the first time she got up enough nerve to confess it.

This was Victoria's second marriage. She had gone from one relationship to another without really dealing with the things in her life, and not knowing the Lord. Going into this marriage, Victoria went in with all her baggage. They were together for a long time; it was a loveless marriage.

About four or five years into the relationship Victoria got radically saved. Victoria says at that moment she knew she got saved and the Lord removed the veil from her eyes. It was like night and day. Even though Victoria got saved, she had no knowledge of what was happening, but she knew something happened and she could feel the presence of God. For the first time Victoria felt like she could really see the sin in her life and the things she had done. In this moment even though it was hard, Victoria could feel the love of the Lord and His presence so strongly. That began a journey for Victoria. In her walk with Him she sees what He had done for her all these years and how He has allowed her to see the reality. That is so important—to see the reality of God and also of what you've done so you can walk in true repentance and receive healing for the things you've done and the choices that you've made.

In sharing this with me, Victoria was amazed at what came out of her mouth in such detail; she realized that she was free because in doing her part, she let the Lord go deep and He brought so much healing to her. She didn't even realize how much until she spoke it out loud that day. All the details.

Toward the end of Victoria sharing with me, something came out that was so life changing and amazing to her. That in the midst of all that chaos—the violence, the angry people, all the hurts that she still carried around inside of her—when she chose life and she chose to have Brittani, it brought LIFE.

You see, at that time Victoria's mom was in despair, she didn't even want to live. She was so depressed that she was just existing, not living. But when Brittani was born, that changed for her. This precious little baby girl, a gift from God, gave Victoria's mother a reason to live. So much so, that she picked herself up. She had purpose and she was a grandmother to Brittani, Victoria's daughter. By Victoria choosing to have her daughter, she brought life to another, her own mother, and gave her hope to live. Not only did this give Victoria's mom a reason to live but brought her healing of being prejudice.

Before Brittani came along her mom was very prejudiced. During Victoria's pregnancy her mom thought that the baby was going to have dark skin; even Victoria thought that. But when Brittani was born, prejudice was broken off her, because she didn't care anymore, because that was her grandbaby. Not only did this precious gift from God bring life in her birth, but also Victoria's choice to give life to her daughter brought life to her mother and broke the spirit of prejudice off her life.

Victoria told me she would need to talk to both her daughter and her mother to see if they were going to be alright with her sharing her story. As she began talking with her mom, before she even got to the part about how it brought her mom life and broke prejudice off her, Victoria's mom said it before she could even finish. Her mother confirmed it all. Even today, Victoria's mom and her daughter Brittani have a special relationship. There is a special bond between the two, because of what God did.

Victoria met with her daughter to make sure it would be OK too for her to share. She told Brittani how her being born, by Victoria choosing life for her, gave her grandmother life, a reason to live after losing two children in tragedy, and it broke prejudice off her grandmother too. As Victoria talked with her, Brittani began getting tears in her eyes. All of this has brought a great sense of redemption into each one of their lives. God is all about redemption, and He is redeeming all that was stolen. Victoria is thankful for all that God has done and all He is continuing to do in hers, her daughter's and mother's life. Victoria is so thankful for her relationship with her mom; she loves her dearly. She is thankful for her daughter Brittani who is beautiful inside and out and how both her mother and her daughter love the Lord.

Victoria's prayer is that as you read her story you will allow the Lord to go deep inside of you and bring healing and restoration to your life. If God can do this for Victoria, her mom, and her daughter Brittani, He surely can do it for you.

Chapter 15

WE ALL HAVE A STORY WE WILL NEVER TELL...

Darkness is a harsh
term don't you think

And yet it dominates
the things I see

It seems that all my
bridges have been burned

But you say "That's exactly
how this grace thing works"
—MUMFORD & SONS

I JUST WANT TO PUT THIS OUT THERE BEFORE WE EVEN GET INTO THE nitty gritty of this chapter. I don't want to be the "abortion" preacher. I wrestled for years trying to decide if I would ever share these stories. I recognize that this chapter *will* be offensive in many circles, and frankly I just don't care. I can't care what people will think any longer. Abortion conversations are not comfortable among the "religious elite." You know, those who have their opinions and theories stowed away into perfectly curated notebooks and repost other people's messages without any gumption or conviction of their own. Religion is a tricky and finicky thing. It's that sneaky thought that makes the crowd love a testimony of the radical redemption of a drug user but makes us shift in our seats when someone repents of adultery or abortion. This chapter is for people searching for life, for those wanting freedom from shame. I hope my journey can unlock you from the bondage of the secret you may have been keeping. The "if anyone found out, I'd be done for" secrets.

Abortion.

Abortion.

Abortion.

Abortion.

For each time I have listed the word above, that is the number of times I sat on a cold metal folding chair filling out paperwork to have an abortion. It was about nine years after having my first abortion that the secret finally came out of my mouth. Did you know that you can make secret agreements with yourself or, even worse, secret agreements with satan? It's true. We do it all the time.

Things like "I'll never date a person who is shorter than me," or "I will lose ten pounds this year." Some of these agreements are good, and some create dark little caves within our souls where we hide away from the world the true testimony of who we are and what God has done. After my first abortion, I subconsciously made one of those little agreements.

"I will never let anyone know I had an abortion."

It was a sticky summer afternoon in Carroll Gardens, Brooklyn. I had just gotten engaged to Parker Green on the beach of Montauk. Parker was the campus pastor of the church I was a part of in Manhattan and we were obsessed with one another. I was all aglow with wedding planning and all of the attention that comes from being newly engaged.

A handful of leaders from our church were being trained in healing ministry and "Sozo." I had always been passionate about praying for people to be set free and was eagerly anticipating the training. A week prior, they had given us a cheaply printed spiral-bound notebook that I had already studied word for word. Before we could begin the training, the team wanted us to first experience prayer ministry for ourselves. At this point,

I had been a born-again Christian for about four years and had been prayed for more times than I could count. I felt a resistance to getting "another" prayer session under my belt, yet I knew I couldn't go on in the training if I didn't sign up.

As I sat in the lead pastor's living room waiting for my appointment, I looked out the floor-to-ceiling windows and watched the F train pass underneath the building. My legs stuck to the leather of the couch while my short, ripped denim Levi's started to cinch at my waist. I waited anxiously for the prayer team to finish their session and call my name. Parker then walked in, confident, with tiny beads of Manhattan sweat running down his forehead onto his neon blue t-shirt. He took a seat next to me and kissed me firmly and asked how I was feeling. "Good, excited, and hoping something crazy happens," I quickly replied.

I then heard the door crack open from the paint sticking to the door frame in the summer heat. An average-height woman with curly brown, unkempt hair called out "Jessi" in a musical tone. I quickly sat up and walked over to the extra bedroom where my appointment would be held. As I sat on the plastic fold-out chair, one of the women in the room handed me a box of tissues. I politely refused and smiled while thanking them both for their time and quickly uttered, "We are really excited to do healing prayer in our church..." when I was smoothly interrupted by unkempt-hair lady who briefly explained how the session would begin.

At first, it felt a bit more like a job interview than a prayer session (if I'm honest). The two women did a thorough background check of obvious unforgiveness issues, irrational fears, and any reoccurring lies I was believing. I always think it is funny when a minister asks, "Are there any lies you are believing?" I guess I think it is silly because how am I to really know? If I am believing it, then I obviously don't know that it is a lie. However, I complied with the questioning and mentioned my ongoing list of people I was forgiving seventy-seven times seven times and the women walked me through a forgiveness prayer for each one. It felt nice to choose to forgive people who hurt me, but there were no Holy Spirit goosebumps and certainly no tears.

As we continued on, I began to feel really confident in my walk with God. I had done the hard work of grieving over things from my past, regularly forgiving others, and constantly talking to leaders about where I was at. I am always described as the "authentic" or "raw" leader, which I appreciated.

The truth is, I just hate secrets. Secrets burn in my chest waiting to come out, which leads to all sorts of problems including gossip and just straight up pissing people off. Yet I wear my "authentic" badge of honor and pride myself on being an open book. As the session was concluding, I started to take mental notes of how I would ask these same questions in a more "provoking" way perhaps. I then noticed the silent woman with the tissue box writing notes on a yellow notepad. I tried to peer over her chubby freckled arms but couldn't make out the scribbles. I boldly asked, "What are you writing?" when she then looked up at me sheepishly.

The two women then exchanged glances, and one said, "Well, that about wraps up your session...unless there is anything else you can think of." I honestly couldn't. I thought they had done a pretty great job until the silent one handed me the piece of paper. On the paper I read: "Kings from Jessi's womb—like Jesse in the Bible."

I felt sick. Why would God bring that up? Why now?

I have found over the last few years that often the things we are hiding are the very things we need to be talking about.

How Secrets Are Born

It was the weekend after my eighteenth birthday. I had just finished my freshman year at the University of Miami. I was home in Huntington, Long Island visiting my parents before heading back to school. I couldn't wait for the summer to be over. My freshman year was what they write teen movies about. I was dating a senior who was president of his fraternity, and while my social status was thriving, my faith was barely hanging on. My nights were filled with 4 a.m. walks back to my dorm room across the sprinkler-soaked intramural fields that separated the fraternity houses from the freshman dorms.

There was not a chance that I was going to wake up early for a campus Bible study or crawl into church and sit in a stiff wooden pew hungover and squinty eyed.

After the whirlwind of my freshman year, I decided to visit a Planned Parenthood in my hometown that summer to get birth control. I nervously walked up to the automatic glass door, afraid of being recognized by one of the country club moms who frequented the shopping complex. Throughout high school, I strongly judged the "trashy" girls who went to Planned Parenthood. Yet here I was wanting to be somewhat responsible in my promiscuous lifestyle. As I filled out the paperwork, my high school friend Bridgett sat next to me and encouraged me that getting birth control was a really mature decision. I agreed, and scribbled a made-up address on the form in fear that my parents would get some kind of newsletter to their conservative home that would expose my irreligious lifestyle.

The woman at the front desk collected my papers and immediately brought me to the back. The Planned Parenthood in my conservative hometown is not exactly overflowing with patients in the waiting room. The town is both traditional in their values and most families are financially well off. The mailboxes that lined the suburban streets never received applications for people seeking medical assistance, and they have a horse and buggy that brings mothers with their children to the stores on Main Street during Christmastime. The entrance sign of my hometown states, "A great place to work, play, and raise a family," and that is not a lie.

As I walked toward the back of the Planned Parenthood, they handed me a cup to fill with urine and place into a stainless-steel metal box in the floral-walled bathroom. I then headed to the examination room, where the doctor asked me the preliminary questions that would qualify me for $30 birth control without my parents' consent and insurance. As I sat on the table, I answered the questions quickly and desperately wanted to be finished. The whole conversation was grating to my Christian upbringing. Discussing with a complete stranger my lifestyle choices felt too exposing, as I had to come face to face with the poor decisions of my last year. As the doctor left the office to write my prescription, I patiently tapped my bare feet on the cold metal chair and read the posters on the wall about various STDs.

I went into the clinic to get a pregnancy test for birth control, and then the nurse came in to tell me that I was in fact pregnant and they could not write me a birth control prescription. Honestly, I freaked out and was so nervous about my parents finding out. My mom raised me as a single parent and I grew up hearing stories of all of the sacrifices she had made for me. I had so many dreams and ambitions, and with this new "news" I saw my entire future quickly going down the drain. I curled up and just began to weep. The nurse didn't skip a beat and quickly gave me my options for abortion. I was past the point to take the morning-after pill and would need to make an appointment for a surgical abortion.

I was only 18 years old and was riddled with fear. Fear of being alone, fear of what people may think, fear of my parents, fear about finances, and fear of losing my boyfriend. These organizations that say they advocate for the rights of women were not advocating for me or for the life of my unborn child. I was never given options for counseling or referred to a clinic to discuss the myriad of options that I had. I could barely decide where to go out for dinner on a Friday night. The decision of what to do with the life of a child was overwhelming. My options were: I could have an abortion or do research to give the child up for adoption.

About a week later, I ended up telling my boyfriend. He freaked out for a few moments and then encouraged me that we would be OK. That we could figure this out together. Hope slowly began to rise. Maybe I could keep the baby and my boyfriend and I could begin a simple and humble life together in Florida. I began running millions of scenarios through my mind and thought maybe I could actually keep this baby. That Sunday, I reluctantly agreed to go to church with my parents. I sat quietly in the pew as the congregation sang "Oh, Ancient of Days." I was in church but couldn't feel further from God or more alone. I slipped out the back door to take "a quick call" from my boyfriend's mom. She was a cool, edgy, liberal mom, and my boyfriend decided to tell her about our "situation" because this was too big for us. On the phone, she lovingly expressed how thankful she was that I was dating her son and how heartbroken she was to hear our news. Without getting into all the details, she strongly encouraged me to go through the simple procedure of an abortion and not "ruin our future."

Alone, Again

My boyfriend agreed with his mother and we were back to the drawing board. I ended up looking back to the resources Planned Parenthood gave me for an in-clinic abortion. The medical staff could make the whole process as "comfortable as possible." The pamphlet encouraged me that I could return to my normal activities following the abortion. I was told "having an abortion is simple, common, and safe." It was much harder to get an abortion after 12 weeks, so if this is a decision I wanted to make, I needed to make it quickly.

I could no longer handle the pressure from my boyfriend, his mother, and the tormenting thoughts that haunted me day in and day out. I made an appointment at the nearest clinic and was in the waiting room within a few days. The waiting room was cold and stale and the wall was lined with metal folding chairs filled with quiet women. No one talked in that waiting room. As I began to fill out my paperwork, I had a panic attack. I couldn't do this. I couldn't go through with this. I would keep the baby, even if I was by myself. I ran to the front desk in tears and handed them my clipboard. I ran into the parking lot and cried out in agony. Why was this happening to me? Why was I so stupid?! I came back into the office and wiped my tears on my jacket sleeve. The woman at the front desk told me that I could not have fits like that because it was "disrupting" the other patients.

It is probably a longer story for another book, but I ended up having the procedure. The process was anything but "simple, common, and safe." After the procedure, I was placed in a cold metal folding chair, bleeding out onto a maxi pad and dozing in and out from the anesthesia. I briefly opened my eyes to see the other women across from me. I felt like cheap cattle in a slaughter house as my body fell forward and my face smashed against the cold white linoleum floor. A nurse came over and propped me up into my chair, readjusted my hospital gown, and snapped her fingers in front of my face. "Wake up, wake up."

But waking up was the very last thing I wanted to do. I wanted to sleep. To slip away. To disappear and never resurface again to face the decision I made. I killed a baby. I killed my baby. They forgot to mention the grief that overwhelms the depths of your soul when you make a decision like that. The fear didn't go away; it only increased and now had a new partner called shame. The door was now officially open for a lifestyle of numbing myself from my thoughts. Cocaine addictions followed. Anything to keep me out and not alone, not in my room, alone with my tormenting thoughts. How could God forgive me? Maybe I didn't want to follow a God who could.

"Abortion is murder. Period," said the young pastor in the car seat in front of me. It took about all of my restraint to not strangle her around the neck with my gold satin headband. There were about eight of us women crammed into a black suburban driving down to Virginia Beach from New York City. I was squished in the third row, which really isn't a row if you ask me. Two of my closest friends were sitting with me, our legs intertwined, resembling the top crust of a homemade apple pie. Our lead pastor was speaking at a women's conference, and a group of us went to enjoy a weekend away in the warm Virginia sun and cheer her on as she preached. The theme for the conference was "Freedom," and many of the women in the car were discussing areas and topics they thought might be brought up. As I was editing a photo on my phone, I overheard someone in the front bring up the topic of abortion. I reached into my bag to pull out my smart water and slowly sipped as I felt my throat closing up and my face begin to get hot.

"Abortion is murder. Period."

Those words rang through my ears, down the veins in my neck, right through the very tips of my fingernails. I lifted my sweatshirt up to my chin, sure that my friends would be able to see my veins heavily pulsating. As adrenaline rushed in, my body was preparing for fight or flight. Yet there I was, stuck in that stupid third row with nowhere to go. I crunched down and hid my phone in between my black leggings and quickly texted my husband Parker about what just happened. I concluded the story with, "This is why I hate Christians and this is why I will never, ever tell anyone."

I quickly saw a grey speech bubble pop up on my phone. Parker replied, "She's an a-hole. Don't let her get to you. She wouldn't know empathy if it punched her in the face." I closed my eyes and slowly pictured myself punching her in the face and saying, "Hi, this is from empathy." I know, really weird visual, but it helped me in that moment.

What pains me is that this is probably not the first conversation like this. I think it is important for me to clarify that I am for women carrying to full term, delivering their baby, and either keeping them or giving them up for adoption. However, the reality is that statistically one in three women are, in fact, having abortions. In hundreds of cases, I have been the first person someone has told that they have had an abortion. All across the globe, pastors, leaders, mentors, and peers are choosing to fight for the lives of the unborn while destroying the lives of the living. We can all do better. Myself included. I can't tell you how many conferences I have been to where everyone watched a beautifully curated video of a former drug addict who turned their life around, became clean, and now follows Jesus. Yet when a woman shares from the stage that she has had an abortion or committed adultery, the room becomes so still that you could hear a communion wafer hit the carpeted ground.

> *Because Jesus was raised from the dead,*
> *we've been given **a brand-new life** and have*
> *everything to live for, **including a future in***
> ***heaven**—and the future starts now! God is*
> *keeping careful watch over us and the future.*
> *The Day is coming when you'll have it all—*
> *life healed and whole* (1 Peter 1:3-5 The
> Message).

This verse stirs something within me. It is a glimpse of what our souls long for. The Gospel is only Good News if you believe it. The truth is, when God created man, we were meant to have an intimate relationship with Him. It says that Adam walked with God in the cool of the day. However, when Eve and Adam were deceived, sin entered the world. I think it is important to note that they were, in fact, deceived. Many of us have the ability to fully access all the things of God, but many of us never get there because of this same deception. When sin entered the world, it separated us from a Holy God. This feels unfair, but as I have learned to love God I understand that this was more unfair to Him than us. The fact that God sent His Son Jesus to come to earth as a man, live a sinless life, die on a cross for my sins, and rise again is a lot to fully accept. Our souls wrestle with whether we are worthy enough to receive this kind of sacrifice. So we accept half-truths while still holding on to our past, our pain, and our own unforgiveness. I believe that for many of us, it is easier to believe in a Jesus who would forgive us for our sins than to follow one who rose from the dead. However, Jesus is in fact alive and ruling and reigning. Peter tells us that because He is alive, we have a new option. Salvation. I want to be clear here. Salvation is so much more than "getting into heaven." It is access, grace, power, and the full ability to live the life God created you for. Salvation is the most amazing miracle to witness, but we settle for less.

Some time later, after that dreadful car ride to the conference, my sister-in-law was running a gathering of female leaders to pray and seek God together before her upcoming conference centering on the topic of freedom. During our time together, we were instructed to write on a postcard something Jesus had us set free from. Going through the motions, I wrote about depression and other things that are more widely accepted within church culture. As we went around the table and shared what we had written, I read my card with confidence as an overcomer. Yet when everyone was finishing up, one of the women had the courage to share something extremely vulnerable.

In the moment of her sharing, I felt the Spirit of God wash over me and whisper, "You need to share your secret." I tried to swallow, but my saliva felt like a million rocks blocking my throat.

With every ounce of courage I had, I spoke up and said, "Wait, I need to say something."

I then unloaded about having an abortion. I hoped that in this place of vulnerability, the other women present would extend forgiveness and mercy for this young girl who made a mistake in her past. As I shared my secret sin, I felt a huge weight come off my heart. The women surrounded me in prayer as I wept and struggled to share.

The next morning, I got coffee with my best friend Gracie. We sat together and I decided to tell her the whole truth. The whole experience of every abortion, every anxiety, shame, fear, and depression that marked the last eight years of my life. Later that evening, my sister-in-law asked me if I would be willing to share that night at a women's ministry event about what God had been setting me free from. I wasn't sure if I could do it. I just told people my secret for the first time yesterday; I didn't know if I had the courage to share with an entire room full of women.

My body shook like a leaf on a tree as the words came out of my mouth on that stage during the event. Afterward, we offered prayer to anyone who needed prayer. Shockingly, I ended up praying for 10-plus women who had had an abortion and had never told anyone until then.

The following week, I decided to share more of my story with a blog post that resulted in thousands of comments, messages, and emails from women and men. So many Christians living with this secret. So many non-Christians wanting nothing to do with church because of the shame of their past. I responded over and over again, offering prayer and reconciliation as I was still on my own journey to freedom.

Fast-forward a few years—my husband and I moved to Orange County, California to plant churches called Salt Churches. They are micro churches that are heavily focused on the Great Commission of reaching people with Jesus and making disciples. With these small, intimate communities that these micro churches foster, there's really no room for secrets. There is no pulpit to hide behind, so to be true to my commitment to vulnerability and authenticity, my church knows my abortion story as I continue to learn to share this part of my past.

Yet as I realized how many women were reaching out to me regarding this topic, I once vented to my husband, "I don't want to be the abortion pastor!" But one morning in prayer, I heard God say to me, "Just love these women the way I have loved you."

The hard truth is that too often people and even leaders in the church say flippant comments about abortion in everyday conversation or on social media without knowing that abortion is the secret story of many in their immediate community. So I am trying to reflect the same grace to others that I needed to hear in that car ride years ago.

So that is what I am trying to do. I am trying to live a life that is a reflection of a Savior who forgives every sin and can free you from shame, fear, and unforgiveness. I want to encourage you to find a place where every person's journey can contribute to the process of healing of those around them as we all become more passionate followers of Jesus. While it isn't always easy, my hope and prayer is that my story can be a catalyst for needed but uncomfortable conversations to be had. Conversations where people take off shame and step into purpose and total and complete freedom.

Chapter 10

The Ultimate Choice

*For he chose us in him before
the creation of the world to be
holy and blameless in his sight.*
—Ephesians 1:4, NIV

Did you know that you were in the very heart of God before the foundations of the earth? In fact, you were a highly thoughtful choice made by the Creator of the universe. Every human being, born and unborn, was chosen by God with specific plans to fulfill. You were in fact God's ultimate choice from the beginning. The Trinity—the Father, the Son, and the Holy Spirit—were present in the beginning, before creation and when you were conceived. *"God said, 'Let us make mankind in our image, in our likeness, so that they may rule over the fish in the sea and the birds in the sky, over the livestock and all the wild animals, and over all the creatures that move along the ground'"* (Gen. 1:26, AMP). No matter the circumstances of your conception, you were chosen by Him for His purpose. Your destiny was in the heart of God even before He delicately knit you together in your mother's womb (see Ps. 139:13, AMP).

Mary's Miraculous Choice

Do you ever wonder what Mary thought as the angel of the Lord told her that she was the one chosen to carry the Savior of the world? Do you think she might have questioned and thought, *This just can't be true?* In Luke 1:34 her response to the angel was, *"How will this be, since I am a virgin"* (NIV). You see, Mary was just a young girl about thirteen years old. I am sure she must have thought, "What will my mother and father think? What will Joseph think of me."

We know that Mary went to visit her cousin Elizabeth. *"Now at this time Mary arose and hurried to the hill country, to a city of Judah (Judea), and she entered the house of Zacharias and greeted Elizabeth. When Elizabeth heard Mary's greeting, her baby leaped in her womb; and Elizabeth was filled with the Holy Spirit and empowered by Him"* (Luke 1:39–41, AMP). Wow, what an effect Jesus had on people even while in His mother's womb. I can't help but think how prophetic this was. As a baby inside his mother's womb, John felt the very presence of the One he would one day baptize. This to me says how important every unborn child is to God. He has a prophetic destiny for each one. Just like John was to become the forerunner for Jesus and his birth was important, so is every baby's life.

Mary ended up staying with Elizabeth for about three months, and then returned to her home and to Joseph with whom she was engaged to be married. When Joseph found out that Mary was pregnant, he didn't want to expose her to public disgrace, so he had made up his mind to divorce her quietly. In those days Jewish custom was that engaged couples were considered married. Do you wonder in today's times with Mary being pregnant, would abortion have been a thought in the back of Joseph's mind? Possibly. All in all, Joseph and Mary made the choice to give life to the one who would one day give them eternal life. And because of their choice, Jesus would make the ultimate choice that affects each and every one of us today.

Jesus' Sacrificial Choice

The time came for the One who caused even John the Baptist to leap inside his mother's womb to make a

sacrificial choice to lay down His life for all mankind—
born and unborn. As it came time for Jesus to face the
ultimate sacrifice of His life, you and I were on His mind.
We became His ultimate choice. The choice to give up
His life for us was the very reason Jesus was born. He
came to give His life so that we can have life, but not only
life, but a more abundant life.

> *For this reason, the Father loves Me, because*
> *I lay down My [own] life so that I may take*
> *it back. No one takes it away from Me, but I*
> *lay it down voluntarily. I am authorized and*
> *have the power to lay it down and to give it*
> *up, and I am authorized and have power to*
> *take it back. This command I have received*
> *from My Father* (John 10:17–18, AMP).

Have you ever felt, unloved, unwanted, ugly, unat-
tractive? Or maybe you've felt hated and you were being
ostracized by a group of people. Possibly you've felt the
sting of death from a wrong choice you made. You hurt
so bad inside that you feel as though pain has become
your lot in life. Maybe shame and guilt have become a
mask that you wear and they have become such a part of
you that it's become your identity. Maybe it's the shame
and guilt of an abortion or maybe it's something else.
Whatever it is, you don't have to wear that mask of shame
and guilt anymore. Jesus has already worn the cloak in
your place. When Jesus died and was resurrected, the
cloak of shame and guilt was removed.

There was an ultimate exchange when Jesus chose to lay down His life for us. Jesus not only suffered physical pain, but also our rejection, shame, and even our guilt. He made the ultimate sacrifice by the choice He made. Jesus was obedient to the purpose of suffering in our place. He suffered for our healing for every sickness and disease known and unknown. And that would have been enough, but that wasn't all He suffered for us.

> *For he shall grow up before him as a tender plant, and as a root out of dry ground: he hath no form or comeliness; and when we shall see him, there is no beauty that we should desire Him. He is despised and rejected by men; a man of sorrows, and acquainted with grief: and we hid as it were our faces from him; he was despised, and we esteemed him not. Surely he hath borne our griefs, and carried our sorrows: yet we esteemed him stricken, smitten by God, and afflicted. But he was wounded for our transgressions, he was bruised for our iniquities: the chastisement of our peace was upon him; and with his stripes we are healed* (Isaiah 53:2–5, KJV).

Where would we be had Mary not chosen to give birth to Jesus? Where would we be had Jesus decided to not be obedient to His heavenly Father, to choose death so that we could live?

Our Destiny & Purpose
Before the Womb

Each one of us makes choices that we can't go back and change. However, because of Jesus's sacrifice we can walk in freedom, sharing with others that what He has done for us, He will do for them too. He created you to walk in freedom and has given you the liberty to make a difference in others' lives.

God never wastes anything we have gone through. Every hurt, all the suffering, every loss we have experienced throughout our lives, He can use. Sometimes we make choices that lead us on a road of heartache, pain, and suffering. Other times we have no control and bad things happen to us. We all know that choices are inevitable every day of our lives. When we wake up and prepare for the day, when we're going to work, school, being stay-at-home parents, whatever the day consists of we have to make choices. Granted, some choices are not a matter of a life or death; however, we might find ourselves facing choices that are a matter of life and death. Those choices do not change our destiny. Before we were formed in our mother's womb, God had a destiny and a purpose already mapped out for us. His plan for us was that we would fulfill everything that He foreordained for us before the foundations of the world.

I love what Kevin Zadai, a wonderful friend in the Lord, says, "We can't fail, because it's already been rigged." You see my destiny was already written before

He even placed me inside my mother's womb. His plan for me was not to harm me or hurt me, but to give me, even as a small two-pound baby girl, a hope and a future. The choices I faced changed the course of my life, yet they led me to exactly what He has called me to, like writing this book so others can know the importance of the journey of the choices. Even though we are faced with hard choices or even when we make the wrong choices, God can bring them full circle to the destiny that He planned for us in the beginning.

Resources

If you or someone you know is in a unplanned pregnancy situation and you need help, please reach out to the following organizations:

Journeys of Choice: Journeysofchoice@gmail.com

Journeys of Choice is an organization that works alongside other pro-life ministries to connect and get women the help they need during an unplanned pregnancy.

National Right to Life: www.nrlc.org

The largest national anti-abortion organization in the United States with affiliates in all 50 states and more than 3,000 local chapters nationwide.

Live Action: www.liveaction.org

Live Action is an American nonprofit anti-abortion organization. Lila Rose founded and leads the group. Live Action is know for its undercover videos taken at Planned Parenthood clinics.

Care Net: www.care-net.org

Founded in 1975, CareNet's mission is acknowledging that every human life begins at conception and is worthy of protection. CareNet offers compassion, hope, and help to anyone considering abortion by presenting them with realistic alternatives and Christ-centered support through our life-affirming network of pregnancy centers, churches, organizations and individuals.

New Life Solutions: www.newlifesolutions.org

New Life Solutions is the ministry head of More2Life youth development program, A Woman's Place medical clinics, Passage of Hope post abortion grief recovery program, and Shepherd's Village single parent ministry.

WE LOVE LIFE/Love Life: www.lovelife.org

Creating a culture where families stop running to abortion centers and start running to the local church.

CITIES 4 LIFE Charlotte: www.cities4life.org

A voice for every unborn child.

MORE Than A Choice: www.abortionsurvivors.org

The Abortion Survivors Network

ABOUT
DONNA GRISHAM

Donna Grisham has a compelling desire to shed light on the truth concerning "choice" during an unplanned pregnancy.

As a post-abortive woman that has been healed from the trauma of rape and abortion, she ministers the healing power of God's heart on this very delicate issue.

Donna resides in the Charlotte, N.C. area and has been with Sid Roth's *It's Supernatural!* for the past 12 years.